Undoubtedly the best-known moral attribute of our heavenly Father is Love. Not the sweet sentimental kind of love that pampers and diminishes self-worth, but agape love, the love that acts, that does what is needed to diminish weaknesses, reduce flaws, heal wounds and build personal character worthy of His divine purpose. That end is most often achieved when men and women experience undeserved and unexplained rejection, mistreatment, weighty responsibility, bruises and trials that challenge resolve and stretch endurance. In this book, tried and tested teacher Mary Wolfe shows that our loving God can be trusted to bring and allow into our lives events, words, and deeds that, although unexplained at the time, work together to mold and unfold in us His character and likeness. My prayer is that our will and attitude humbly submit to receive God's engrafted message conveyed through the lessons in *Trusting God with the Unexplained.*

Sidney L Poe, Ph.D.

TRUSTING GOD *with the Unexplained*

TRUSTING GOD *with the* *Unexplained*

MARY W. WOLFE

ISBN: 9781521871508

DEDICATION

I dedicate this book to my four daughters, Debbie, Tamara, Bethany and Stacey, and my grandson, Jon Laurence Lachney - all faithful critics and my most loyal supporters. I could not have accomplished even this small a project without their encouragement, editing, suggestions, and talents. Also my husband, Larry Wolfe, who has remained steady in the storms of life and has trusted God with me through it all.

CONTENTS

FOREWORD

The Gospel writer, Luke, spoke of the "certain women" who followed Jesus in the days of His earthly ministry and "ministered unto him of their substance." One of those women was named Mary. While her story is quite different from Mary Wolfe's, they both share a testimony of God's enabling grace.

Mary Wolfe is an astute student of the Word. She is a woman of prayer. She walks in the Spirit that indwells her. She has experienced firsthand "the unexplained" that God and life often hand to us. As her Pastor for decades, I can attest to the fact that she has lived what she has written.

Mary is a gifted teacher and has for many years, in many roles, taught lessons from the Word at The Pentecostals of Alexandria and beyond. She is outstanding in her study and in her presentation. Her research skills are impeccable. She has often served as a researcher for my sermons and projects. Be it in a small group setting, in a class setting, as a mentoring tool, or even for personal Bible study, you will find Trusting God With The Unexplained to be of immeasurable value to you.

Mary shares with her readers the journey to trusting God even with the unexplained. You will find here more than a personal testimony, rather an anointed guide built on Biblical truth, wrapped in faith that ever leads to that final relinquishment that is pure trust in Him.

Anthony Mangun, Senior Pastor,
The Pentecostals of Alexandria

PREFACE

Why suffering? Why trouble? Why hardships? These are questions that have destroyed the faith of many. We are troubled by the unfair distribution of suffering in the world. Question marks turn into painful hooks into our hearts, barbs that pierce our very soul. This book has seven Bible studies to address these questions that have perplexed many. Can we victoriously trust God when all hell breaks loose in our lives? What about the daily crises - large and small - of life? Whom should we blame when tragedy strikes? Can we ever recover from the bruises and hurts that we have experienced? Can we finish our life's journey with our faith intact?

The seven chapters of this book are from notes of Bible studies I have taught over the years. These lessons were birthed not only from diligent study on trusting God, but also from life experiences, most of them frustrating and mundane, but some tragic and devastating.

Although my finite mind will never fully grasp God's ways, the longer I live and the more I delve into His word the more I am convinced that all things truly do work together for good and that there is purpose and reason to what may seem just chaos. Certainly not all things are good and not all things are from God. In fact, Satan hinders us as he did Paul (I Thessalonians 2:18). But there is nothing that happens to us that God cannot use, there is nothing the body suffers that the soul cannot profit by. One thing has become my bedrock: God's very essence is love! Love can and will make the best of every circumstance of life if we let it. God will use the dark threads in our life to weave a picture of deliverance and victory for all to see.

ACKNOWLEDGMENTS

Mark Twain noted, "What a good thing Adam had. When he said a good thing, he knew nobody had said it before." Although I present this as "by Mary Wolfe," in the reality of teaching over six decades, I have used many sources, integrating materials into my lectures so often that the lines are blurred between what is original and what is inspired from others. I have sat under some of the greatest teachers and preachers of our times, noting their insights into spirituality and building my own perspective. Sitting under and working with giants like Vesta Mangun, Anthony Mangun, T. F. Tenney, and Terry Shock have indelibly printed their spirits on my work. Dear friends and Bible scholars like Larry Clark and Roger Skluzacek challenge me to daily gain new awareness and intimacy with scripture.

If I fail to acknowledge any inspired ideas, I hope those from whom I have borrowed will feel honored rather than slighted. Many ideas will reflect the ground-breaking work of A. W. Tozer and E. M. Bounds, Herbert Lockyer and Rabbi Joseph Telushkin, as their writings help direct my growth as a teacher. The writings of Amy Carmichael and E. Stanley Jones have also influenced me greatly.

I present nothing but what I have received through divine inspiration or human effort, and I gladly acknowledge all those from which I gather my own voice.

Also, my gratitude goes out to those who have openly received my teachings and expressed benefit of integrating into their own teachings. You ministers and teachers give me the purpose of moving forward from speaking to writing.

Mary Wolfe

Within the maddening maze of things,
When tossed by storm and flood,
To one fixed trust my spirit clings;
I know that God is good!
I know not what the future hath
Of marvel or surprise,
Assured alone that life and death
His mercy underlies.

John Greenleaf Whittier, 1867

TRUSTING GOD IN DOTHAN

Dothan: A portrait of suffering and a portrait of mighty deliverance. Sooner or later, in every believer's life, these two Dothans will come.

Dothan was mentioned only twice in the Old Testament: It was significant in the lives of Joseph and Elisha.

Joseph's Experience in Dothan*:*

> *And the man said, They are departed hence; for I heard them say, Let us go to Dothan. And Joseph went after his brethren, and found them in Dothan. And when they saw him afar off, even before he came near unto them, they conspired against him to slay him. And they said one to another, Behold, this dreamer cometh. Come now therefore, and let us slay him, and cast him into some pit, and we will say, Some evil beast hath devoured him: and we shall see what will become of his dreams.* *Genesis 37:17-20*

A vivid picture of suffering: In verse 23, they stripped him, in verse 24, they cast him into a pit, in verse 28, they sold him into slavery. Betrayal, rejection, violence, trauma.

Elisha's Experience in Dothan:

> *And he said, Go and spy where he is, that I may send and fetch him. And it was told him, saying, Behold, he is in Dothan. Therefore sent he thither horses, and chariots, and a*

great host: and they came by night, and compassed the city about. And when the servant of the man of God was risen early, and gone forth, behold, an host compassed the city both with horses and chariots. And his servant said unto him, Alas, my master! how shall we do? And he answered, Fear not: for they that be with us are more than they that be with them. And Elisha prayed, and said, LORD, I pray thee, open his eyes, that he may see. And the LORD opened the eyes of the young man; and he saw: and, behold, the mountain was full of horses and chariots of fire round about Elisha.

And when they came down to him, Elisha prayed unto the LORD, and said, Smite this people, I pray thee, with blindness. And he smote them with blindness according to the word of Elisha. And Elisha said unto them, This is not the way, neither is this the city: follow me, and I will bring you to the man whom ye seek. But he led them to Samaria. And it came to pass, when they were come into Samaria, that Elisha said, LORD, open the eyes of these men, that they may see. And the LORD opened their eyes, and they saw; and, behold, they were in the midst of Samaria. And the king of Israel said unto Elisha, when he saw them, My father, shall I smite them? shall I smite them? And he answered, Thou shalt not smite them: wouldest thou smite those whom thou hast taken captive with thy sword and with thy bow? set bread and water before them, that they may eat and drink, and go to their master. And he prepared great provision for them: and when they had eaten and drunk, he sent them away, and they went to their master. So the bands of Syria came no more into the land of Israel. 2 Kings 6:13-23

A picture of mighty deliverance…"the bands of Syria came no more into the land of Israel."

In each life that follows after the Lord there will be, sooner or later, these two Dothans. Sometimes there will be glorious interventions. Our God will be to us a God of deliverance upon the mountains round about us. Sometimes we shall see only bare blue sky, empty hillsides, nothing but a pit.

All of us have had our miracles of deliverance. All of us have had times when we suffer misery, betrayal, pain and we wonder, "My God, why?" Like David we cry: Why are thou so far from helping me and from the words of my roaring.

There is a question that has destroyed the faith of many. Why do bad things happen to good people? We are troubled by the unfair distribution of suffering in the world. Life is not fair. Question marks turn into hooks into our heart, barbs that pierce our very soul.

The wisest man that ever lived was bewildered by even small injustices: *"I have seen servants upon horses and princes walking as servants upon the earth."* Ecclesiastes 10:7

The suffering of godless, evil persons presents no mystery; overtaken in pain and suffering, we feel they reap what they have sown. But Paul told us, *"For we know the whole creation groans and travails in pain up to this moment."* Romans 8:22

Think of 17-year-old Joseph - a young man sheltered by his father, a young man with dreams, a young man trying to do right, endeavoring to live in accordance with God's will for life, a young man strongly adverse to indulging in sin. (See Genesis 37:2) He certainly must have been mystified when his hopes were crushed and his dreams dashed. "If there is a personal God who loves me, why did He not save me from this tragedy?"

The psalmist said of Joseph: "*... who was sold for a servant:*

Whose feet they hurt with fetters: he was laid in iron: Until the time that his word came: the word of the LORD tried him. Psalm 105:17-19. Where were the mountains full of angels?

Paul tells us in Romans 8:28: *And we know that all things work together for good to them that love God, to them who are the called according to his purpose.* Note: Not all things are for our good. Not even all things are the will of God. But if we love God and are called according to his purpose, all things work together (even what Satan sends our way).

Many years later, Joseph said of his Dothan experience: *But as for you, ye thought evil against me; but God meant it unto good, to bring to pass, as it is this day, to save much people alive. Now therefore fear ye not: I will nourish you, and your little ones. And he comforted them, and spake kindly unto them.* Genesis 50:20

They meant it for evil --- but God turned it around. Consider that in Joseph's pit, the very thing he had dreamed about was being brought to pass. He could have rebelled. Pseudofaith says, "I don't accept this.." Real faith says: "Whatever happens, it is not going to get me down. It is working for my good."

If Joseph had let Dothan make him bitter, a total of 70 souls would have had nowhere to turn to in their hour of desperation. Even the plan of salvation would have been in jeopardy for the ancestry of the Messiah was in danger of extinction by starvation.

Consider the following axioms:

•There is nothing that can happen to me as child of God that God cannot use.

•"Make the devil sorry he ever did that to you." Vesta Mangun

•"There is nothing the body suffers that the soul may not

profit by." George Meredith.
•Anything that draws me closer to God can't be all bad.
•Greatest good can come of our greatest evil. (Who was responsible for Judas betraying Jesus. "Satan entered into the heart of Judas... " but Jesus' crucifixion was the best thing that could have happened for me.)

Consider: Why did God allow such a godly man as Stephen, full of faith and Holy Ghost, to be brutally stoned to death by a vicious mob? Where was the God that intervened miraculously for Peter with an angel that opened the jailhouse for him. God neither slumbers or sleeps. He is all knowing, all powerful... so did He care?

Why suffering? Why trouble? Why hardships? There are two traps: On the one hand, we can mistakenly believe that all suffering gets you points; penance/suffering is an end in itself; i.e., the more you suffer, the more spiritual you are (hence medieval bed of nails, hair shirts/flaying one's self). Just as erroneous is the belief that "*Gain is godliness...*" (1 Timothy 6:5) and that if one is suffering, he must be out of the will of God, the belief that someone must have sinned or this wouldn't be. This was the fallacy in the thinking of Job's friends. This is the fallacy in the thinking of so many Christians today. The disciples also thought this way when confronted with a blind man in the gospel of John. *"Who did sin, this man or his parents, that he should be born blind?" Jesus answered, Neither hath this man sinned, nor his parents: but that the works of God should be made manifest in him.* John 9:2,3

In Luke 13:4, 5, when the disciples heard of tragedies in their day, they asked Jesus about the Galilaeans, whose blood Pilate had mingled with their sacrifices. *"And Jesus answering said unto them, Suppose ye that these Galilaeans were sinners above all the Galilaeans, because they suffered such things? I tell you, Nay..." Or those eighteen, upon whom the tower in Siloam fell, and slew them, think ye that they were sinners above all men that dwelt in Jerusalem? I tell you, Nay..."*

Even it was prophesied in Isaiah 53 of Jesus: *We esteemed Him smitten of God and afflicted.*

Suffering has no respect of persons. The sun shines impartially on the evil and good. Rain falls impartially on the evil and good. Your picnic will get rained on. Pain overtakes without discrimination saint and sinner alike. *Many are the afflictions of the righteous: but the LORD delivereth him out of them all.* Psalm 34:19 Sometimes deliverance will come as to Elisha, immediate, complete, the enemy routed. *"The bands of Syria came no more."* Sometimes it will be a more drawn out affair - 13 years for Joseph. Sometimes it will take eternity to balance the scales. Eventually though... *"the LORD delivereth him out of them all."*

As Job we must say, *"... all the days of my appointed time will I wait, till my change come."* Job 14:14 We know *"...weeping may endure for a night, but joy cometh in the morning."* Psalm 30:5 *Be sober, be vigilant; because your adversary the devil, as a roaring lion, walketh about, seeking whom he may devour: Whom resist stedfast in the faith, knowing that the same afflictions are accomplished in your brethren that are in the world. But the God of all grace, who hath called us unto his eternal glory by Christ Jesus, after that ye have suffered a while, make you perfect, stablish, strengthen, settle you.* 1 Peter 5:8-10

After you have suffered awhile: Poverty, cancer, tragedy, death. Flat tires, fender benders, sewers stopped up. Ambulances, cemeteries, hospitals, funeral homes.

Suffering, adversity, trouble, if we let it, can draw us closer to God, give us a revelation of Him, make us more effective in our service to Him. *("Make you perfect, stablish, strengthen, settle you").* Or it will make us bitter, faithless, indrawn, engrossed in our tragedies, counting our booboos with self-pity or self-accusation. Our reaction to the problem then becomes the problem.

Paul wrote from prison to the church at Thessalonica: *But we, brethren, being taken from you for a short time in presence, not in heart, endeavoured the more abundantly to see your face with great desire. Wherefore we would have come unto you, even I Paul, once and again; but Satan hindered us.* 1Thessalonians 2:17,18. Note, "even I Paul." He really wanted to! He really tried! If Satan could hinder Paul, he certainly can hinder us.

Paul could have sat and pouted and regretted what could have been. He didn't get to go help the church at Thessalonica. However, he wrote 1 and 2 Thessalonians to them and these words have helped millions since. *But I would ye should understand, brethren, that the things which happened unto me have fallen out rather unto the furtherance of the gospel.* Philippians 1:12

I was privileged to become acquainted personally with a native Ethiopian minister's wife. She was no illiterate heathen; she was well-educated, attractive, and knew six languages. At one point in their mission work her baby was taken from her arms by soldiers and flung against a hard surface and died. There were times she was imprisoned for the gospel.

Years later, she had the opportunity to come to the United States, and we were showing her around in a big city, visiting malls, restaurants, etc. Although her home country, Ethiopia, is synonymous with poverty, famine, repression, she made it clear that she would not want to live here. She told us, "You of necessity are all too caught up in this life." While here, she got a phone call from Ethiopia and came out beaming with the expression, “Good news!” We thought, “Oh, did someone give lots of money to your work; was a head of state converted?” “No, forty church members had been arrested.” "That's good news?" The answer was, “Yes, always significant substantial church growth follows when persecution increases."

When I was an adolescent, there was a minister who made a great impression on me: S. L. Wise, District Superintendent of Louisiana District of the United Pentecostal Church. He suffered from rheumatoid arthritis for years and for the last few years of his life he was bedridden. Many thought he could be so much more effective with his ministry if he were not in a wheelchair, if he were not suffering. However, I, like many others, may have forgotten the messages he preached, but I will never forget him living out the scripture: *...so now also Christ shall be magnified in my body, whether it be by life, or by death.* Philippians 1:20

Suffering will put either a window or a mirror in one's life - a mirror to become preoccupied with self, or a window to feel for others. (Ezekiel: *I came to them of the captivity … and I sat where they sat...* Ezekiel 3:15)

Who comforteth us in all our tribulation that we may be able to comfort them which are in any trouble by the comfort wherewith we ourselves are comforted of God. 2 Corinthians 1:4

Suffering can give us sympathy, empathy, compassion that is only born from the womb of experience.

~You can only help others in proportion to what you yourself have suffered. The greater the price, the more you can help others. The lesser the price, the less you can help others. As you go through fiery trials, testings, afflictions, persecutions, conflicts--as you let the Holy Spirit work the dying of Jesus in you--life will flow out to others, even the life of Christ. ~ Watchman Nee

Songwriter, Fannie Crosby, was blinded at six months by a mistake of a doctor. Bitter? No, she wrote, "Blessed assurance, Jesus is mine, oh what a foretaste of glory divine." Third verse: "Perfect submission, all is at rest; I in my Savior am happy and blest, watching and waiting, looking above, filled with his goodness, lost in his love." She also wrote this poem:

O what a happy soul am I, although I cannot see. I am resolved that in this world contented I will be. How many blessings I enjoy that other people don't. To weep and sigh because I'm blind, I cannot and I won't.

One consolation to her was: "Just think, the first thing I shall see will be His face."

A minister whose wife had forsaken him wrote the hymn:

No one ever cared for me like Jesus; There's no
other friend so kind as He. No one else could take
the sin and darkness from me; O how much He
cared for me.

Talk about taking a lemon and making lemonade! Satan will think again before he gives another lemon to someone with that kind of grace. *Beloved, think it not strange concerning the fiery trial which is to try you, as though some strange thing happened unto you: But rejoice, inasmuch as ye are partakers of Christ's sufferings; that, when his glory shall be revealed, ye may be glad also with exceeding joy.* 1 Peter 4:12, 13

Paul who "suffered the loss of all things," penned these words: *For I reckon that the sufferings of this present time are not worthy to be compared with the glory which shall be revealed in us. Romans 8:18.*

Heads we win. . . tails we win. Riches we win... poverty we win. Success we win... failure we win. Healthy we win... sick we win. For me to live is Christ... and to die is gain.

Lazarus, a close friend of Jesus and of his disciples, was sick and word was sent to Jesus. Jesus delayed going. *"Then said Jesus unto them plainly, Lazarus is dead. And I am glad for your sakes that I was not there, to the intent ye may believe; nevertheless let us go unto him.* John 11:14, 15.

Can you imagine their confusion: "Lazarus is dead and I am glad for your sakes I was not there"? Then Jesus wept with them at the cemetery. He knew what was about to happen. He knew it was for their good. He knew their faith would soar. However, like a parent looking on when their baby is getting an injection - knowing the pain will only last for a moment, knowing the outcome is for its ultimate good - they still feel the injection with him.

At one point, Jesus said of His actions, *"...What I do thou knowest not now, but thou shalt know hereafter."* John 13:7 If we could only remember this one thing in our sufferings.

I recall a traumatic time in my life. We were establishing a new home missions church. Our house caught fire in the middle of the night. We barely escaped ourselves. We stood barefooted in freezing weather, outside at 3:00 am watching our belongings go up in flames. At the time it seemed like the end of the world to me. Looking back now, I can see the good that came out of it, prayers that were answered not only for us personally but for the work there.

When my dad died, it was devastating to our family.

One grandson, not wayward, but perhaps a little nonchalant about his commitment to God, took it to heart and decided he would do his best to fill his shoes. He made a consecration, became a faithful minister, and has preached to thousands, influencing many young people for Christ. Was that the reason my dad died? No, it was his time, but God brought this good out of it.

It has been well said: Trust is faith where we cannot track, following Him even when we cannot fathom His purpose in delaying to come to our aid.

Life deals some pretty devastating blows. You will feel battered, bruised, maybe even down for the count, punch drunk. Some of you have had some really hard knocks; you have been kicked in the teeth by life. Maybe you have scars from abuse as a child, molestation, traumatic experiences as young adults, dysfunctional families. Life has not been fair. Perhaps the love of a mother or dad was denied you, maybe the love of a companion. You have battled with one of two rationalizations: Either God wasn't there when you needed Him, God let you down, God was unjust, or you deserved the pain and suffering; somehow you brought it on yourself; you are no good; you are worthless. Given those two rationales, you have a choice: You can hate God for sending suffering that you did not deserve, or you can hate yourself for deserving such a fate.

Both are lies of Satan: God didn't send it. You did not deserve it. Satan, the god of this world, is a murderer, a liar, a roaring lion. You will believe his lies and be Satan's trophy or you can be a mighty monument to the grace of God.

Jesus said offenses would come. Jesus said there would be earthquakes, famines, pestilences, fearful sights, some shall be hated, betrayed "*but it shall turn to you for a testimony.*" Luke 21:10-17 This is true on a global scale, and this is true on a personal scale.

Trust God with the unexplained. Trust God in Dothan. Trust Him with mighty deliverance. Trust Him with unexplained suffering. What He does thou knowest not now, but thou shalt know hereafter!

If we let Him, God will use the dark threads in our life to weave a picture of deliverance for all to see.

Romans 8 is a treatise on this very subject. It closes with the following verses: *Nay, in all these things we are more than conquerors through him that loved us. For I am persuaded, that neither death, nor life, nor angels, nor principalities, nor powers, nor things present, nor things to come, Nor height, nor depth, nor any other creature, shall be able to separate us from the love of God, which is in Christ Jesus our Lord.* Romans 8:37-39

Recommended Reading and Resources

Carmichael, Amy. Rose from Brier. London: SPCK Publishing, 1933. Print

Lockyer, Herbert. Dark Threads the Weaver Needs: The Problem of Human Suffering. Grand Rapids, MI: Baker Publishing Group, 1995. Print.

Why Doesn't God Do Something? Message By: T.F. Tenney (2008). http://focusedlight.net/bookstore (CD $10.00)

Trusting God in Dothan Workbook as a PDF file is available on request to mwolfe242@aol.com ($5.00)

Trusting God in Dothan PowerPoint available on request to mwolfe242@aol.com (no charge)

LIFE APPLICATION

1. Contrast Stephen's persecution with Peter's deliverance. What great good came to the church as a result of Stephen's persecution? Was Peter delivered from jail every time? What was a result of his adverse experiences?

2. Now consider and contrast the lives of James and John.

3. Contrast the ends of Elijah's (2 Kings 2:11) and Elisha's (2 Kings 13:14) lives. Did this mean that Elijah was more spiritual than Elisha? Who performed the most miracles throughout his life?

4. Study Romans 8, a treatise on trusting God, particularly the closing verses. Romans 8:37-39 *"Nay, in all these things we are more than conquerors through him that loved us. For I am persuaded, that neither death, nor life, nor angels, nor principalities, nor powers, nor things present, nor things to come, Nor height, nor depth, nor any other creature, shall be able to separate us from the love of God, which is in Christ Jesus our Lord."* Now consider verse 28, which states: *"And we know that all things work together for good to them that love God, to them who are the called according to his purpose."* It is important that we quote this scripture (Romans 8:28) correctly. Are all things good? Are all things sent by God?. This precious promise is to what particular group of people? How does this affect us?

5. Does God's favor give us immunity against afflictions, disasters, and trouble? Thinking about the previous question, consider how it applies to the life of Mary, the mother of Jesus (Luke 1:30 and Luke 2:34-35), and Daniel (Daniel 9:23, Daniel 10:11, 19 and Daniel 6:16).

6. Consider Philippians 4:19, which says, "But my God shall supply all your need according to his riches in glory by Christ

Jesus." How might we, at times, falsely interpret the scripture to mean God will meet all of our "physical needs?"

7. Paul said himself in 2 Corinthians 11:25-27: *"Thrice was I beaten with rods, once was I stoned, thrice I suffered brethren; In weariness and painfulness, in watchings often shipwreck, a night and a day I have been in the deep; In journeyings often, in perils of waters, in perils of robbers, in perils by mine own countrymen, in perils by the heathen, in perils in the city, in perils in the wilderness, in perils in the sea, in perils among false, in hunger and thirst, in fastings often, in cold and nakedness."* Can you think of instances in the scripture where Paul's physical "needs" were not supplied all the time?

8. Can the "want" of natural things sometimes be conducive to our spiritual health? If so, in what ways?

9. The church of Smyrna was one church in Revelation about which Jesus had only good things to say, but He said to them, *"I know thy [. . .] poverty."* Read Revelation 2:9-10. What was Jesus's exhortation to them?

10. Luke 21:16-18 says, *"And ye shall be betrayed both by parents, and brethren, and kinsfolks, and friends; and some of you shall they cause to be put to death. And ye shall be hated of all men for my name's sake. But there shall not an hair of your head perish."* How can we harmonize verse 16: *"some of you shall they cause to be put to death,"* and verse 18, *"But there shall not an hair of your head perish?"*

NOTES:

____

____

____

____

____

THAT WHICH COMETH UPON ME DAILY

"Beside those things that are without, that which cometh upon me daily, the care of all the churches."

Of the Jews five times received I forty stripes save one. Thrice was I beaten with rods, once was I stoned, thrice I suffered shipwreck, a night and a day I have been in the deep; In journeyings often, in perils of waters, in perils of robbers, in perils by mine own countrymen, in perils by the heathen, in perils in the city, in perils in the wilderness, in perils in the sea, in perils among false brethren; In weariness and painfulness, in watchings often, in hunger and thirst, in fastings often, in cold and nakedness. Beside those things that are without, that which cometh upon me daily, the care of all the churches. 2 Corinthians 11:24-28

Sometimes we can deal with tragedies, serious sickness, trauma, true hardship easier than "that which cometh daily, the care of all…" The aggravations, the frustrations, the troubles seem without rhyme or reason, not so much fiery trials - but stinging fire ants. The cares of life choke out the good seed. It's not that life is so very bad, we think it just could be so much better. We deal with life: Misunderstandings, sewer stopped up, long lines at the store, a fender bender, flat tires, a mistake in the checkbook, audit by IRS. Pressure, stress, anxiety escalates. "When it rains it pours..." LIFE IS SO DAILY!!! It seems that Murphy's Law rules: If anything can go wrong, it will. We agree with the crude bumper sticker: "Bad stuff " happens! We learn to expect it!

One of the first things you learned to say as a baby is

"Uh-oh!!" You drop things. You break things. You fall down. "Uh-oh!" Two small syllables with large meanings: So much for plan A. That's the way the cookie crumbles. That's the way the ball bounces.

The older we get and the more knowledge and experience we have, it should be the more we are able to distinguish momentary difficulty from serious trouble, the more we should know something is "uh-oh" and not "911." We ask the toddler who is wailing and screaming, "Is it hospital bad?" My two-year-old grandson said "ouch" for any small thing that went wrong. An older cousin said, "He doesn't know what 'ouch' means, does he?"

A child gets upset and pitches a fit. To an adolescent, relatively minor upsets can seem like the end of the world. Then as adults, after years of "don't make a mountain out of a molehill," "don't cry over spilled milk," "you must roll with the punches," "don't sweat the small things," hopefully we achieve perspective. We learn that "If we treat every situation as a life and death matter, we will die a thousand times…" Life as we know it in our intricate civilization can be deadly unless we learn to distinguish the things that matter from those that do not. It is never the major things that destroy us, but invariably the multitude of trivial things which are mistakenly thought to be of major importance. These can be so overwhelming that unless we get out from under them, they will crush us body and soul.

One wisely stated, "You can tell the maturity of a man by the size of things that upset him." What upsets me? What causes me to get "bent out of shape? What is it that angers me? Is it perceived slights to my ego or real injustice? We choose our actions and reactions. The decision is ours. We decide to be a thermostat and regulate the emotional temperature around us or to be a thermometer and rise and fall with the heated or cooled atmosphere, to be affected by every wind that blows. If the environment is hot and angry, I blow my top. If others are cool and aloof, I get icy. Will I act or react? I can resolve: "I will let no man's conduct determine mine."

Jesus did not react to personal attacks when people doubted and belittled him based on his hometown and family background. *"Can there any good thing come out of Nazareth?"* Jesus' response, with perhaps a shrug of His shoulders, was: *"A prophet is without honor in own country."* Would we have been tempted to preach a message on prejudice? Would we have said, "On my mother's side, I'm a descendent of David; on my Father's side, royalty, King of Kings." What did get His attention were important things: When the temple was being used improperly, not as a house of prayer (Luke 19:46), when the religious leaders "hindered others." (Matthew 23:13), hypocrisy (Matthew 23:14) and religious leaders twisting the Word of God. (Matthew 23:16-17, 23-24).

Do I live on a superficial plane? What really concerns me? Am I shallow in what I expect out of life? Am I shallow in what I expect out of a day? Am I shallow in what I expect out of Saviour? Am I shallow in what I expect out of God? Do I live for the superficial: Emotionally? Spiritually?

Think for a moment of the last time you were really upset. You lost your cool, maybe blew your stack. Can you even remember what it was about? Now looking back, was it an uh-oh or 911 moment. Was it something that really mattered in the scheme of life? Will it matter a year from now? Or even a week?

> "A trial comes, disappointments happen. In a few days, months, years, we shall have forgotten it. But the way we meet the trial belongs to eternity. It will matter 10,000 years hence whether we were conquered by that temptation to faithlessness, impatience, or worry." Amy Carmichael

Because of the problem we have magnifying the cares of life, our concept of a Saviour/Messiah/hero is often shallow. We envision our God to be some kind of Santa Claus. "He knows when you've been bad or good, so be good for goodness sake. You better watch out…" We have an image of a benevolent old gentleman, one that you can climb in his lap and give him your gift list; if you are good for a year, you'll get what you want. "Give me, give me…" ; rewarding the good, overlooking the bad.

Have you ever thought about the heroes we create? Superman flying in to right wrongs. The Lone Ranger who comes to the rescue. The Hulk who gets angry at injustice, "that's not right" and takes care of it with a wham/bam. As humans, when we create a "redeemer" - a savior - we keep him safely distant in his faraway castle: Coming to our rescue, giving us our desires, swooping down, not really involved, fixing things – and going on, leaving us alone.

Then we get the frame of mind, "What kind of God let's bad things happen to good people." Like Gideon, we wallow in self-pity and think "If the Lord be with us, why then is all this befallen us?" The God of the Bible is something much deeper. Only God would or could come up with this concept - what we would not dare dream, a relationship. *" … He will dwell with them, and they shall be his people, and God himself shall be with them, and be their God."* Revelation 21:3

In fact, this is our very purpose: God created man for his love. Love is one thing that no one – not even God Himself – can command. It is a free gift – or valueless.

God created man truly free to choose. To give us the ability to make our choice to love him, to live for him, he has to leave us free to choose to do right or to do wrong. *I call heaven and earth to record this day against you, that I have set before you life and death, blessing and cursing: therefore choose life, that both thou and thy seed may live.* Deuteronomy 30:19

To make men free, God had to limit himself. He would have to step back and allow that free will to operate. He gave us dominion and as we are His adult children, he awaits/needs/desires our permission to be involved in our situations. If I want to hurt someone – or hurt my own future – God will not always intervene to keep me from doing so - or conversely if someone chooses to hurt me. God has set himself a limit that he will not intervene to take away our freedom of choice. Of course, certain rewards are built in the system and certain punishments are automatic (with promiscuity, excesses, not doing right). There are blessings and cursings that are inevitable.

We think if we ran the universe, there would be no flat tire on the way to do a good deed, no lost jobs if one paid their tithes. There would be no rejection from others when one did his best. We envision in a perfectly fair world morality would operate according to fixed laws, like the laws of nature. However, if this world ran according to fixed, perfectly fair rules, there would be no freedom. A fair world would punish sin swiftly and surely: Extend your hand to shoplift, you'd get an electric shock. Do good, be honest on your income tax, you would be rewarded, maybe win the sweepstakes. *Because sentence against an evil work is not executed speedily, therefore the heart of the sons of men is fully set in them to do evil.* Ecclesiastes 8:11.

In the millennium, it will be so. *And it shall come to pass, that every one that is left of all the nations which came against Jerusalem shall even go up from year to year to worship the King, the LORD of hosts, and to keep the feast of tabernacles. And it shall be, that whoso will not come up of all the families of the earth unto Jerusalem to worship the King, the LORD of hosts, even upon them shall be no rain. And if the family of Egypt go not up, and come not, that have no rain; there shall be the plague, wherewith the LORD will smite the heathen that come not up to keep the feast of tabernacles. This shall be the punishment of Egypt, and the punishment of all nations that come not up to keep the feast of tabernacles.* Zechariah 14:16-19

But that is not what God is trying to accomplish right now. He is not looking for zombies, robots, doing what is right out of instinct – or because of benefits derived. If this world ran according to fixed, perfectly fair rules, there would be no freedom. We would act rightly because of immediate gain. Selfish motives would taint every act of goodness. God wants us to love him freely, even when immediate return is not evident. In fact, he wants us to cleave to him as Job did even when we have every reason to deny him. His purpose is to take a bride for his namesake - a soul mate for eternity, someone that loves Him heart, soul, mind and strength, "to have and to hold, from this day forward, for better or for worse, for richer or for poorer, in sickness and in health …"

There is a contest in the spiritual realm: Satan tries to convince us that man is not really free. He claimed that Job loved God for reasons, that he had ulterior reasons. *"Does Job serve you for nought?"* Take away the positive rewards, Satan challenged, and watch Job turn on you *Doth Job fear God for nought? Hast not thou made an hedge about him, and about his house, and about all that he hath on every side? thou hast blessed the work of his hands, and his substance is increased in the land. But put forth thine hand now, and touch all that he hath, and he will curse thee to thy face.* (Job 1:9-11)

Satan sneers: Every man has his price, *"all that a man hath will he give for his life."* In other words, man's first concern is himself, his own self-interest, that no one will love God just because …. that they want a Santa Claus, a magic genie, a superman. He believes that no one would love God better than they love themselves. Satan is the accuser of the brethren: "If it weren't for the daily benefits… they'd be mine." Satan is jealous of the bride of Christ. While our Saviour woos with His love, Satan is enticing, seducing, beguiling. Satan is telling God, "She just loves you for what you will do for her, the superficial, the trivial. She has her price… her ego, her skin, " "all that a man hath…"

Satan is the third party of the eternal triangle, accusing us to God: Take that away – they'll curse you. They don't really love you. Accusing God to us: "Hath God said…?," "thou shalt not surely die," "it is too hard," "God doesn't really love you or He wouldn't require this of you… He would not let you suffer this. He would rescue you." Satan is promising us benefits now – "daily." "Bow down and worship me and you can have kingdoms today. Eat the forbidden fruit and you will be like God. Disobey! Break the rules. Have your cake and eat it too. I'll make it easier. God doesn't want you to have any fun, any power."

God's purpose is to take a bride for His name's sake, to find out who loves Him for Himself and not for what he will do, someone that will love Him "just because." *"Jesus answered them and said, Verily, verily, I say unto you, Ye seek me, not because ye saw the miracles, but because ye did eat of the loaves, and were filled.* " John 6:26

Don't get it wrong: He loves to do for His betrothed, His chosen bride. What is important to me is important to Him. *"Casting all your care for He careth for you."* I Peter 5:7. His first miracle was performed to prevent the embarrassment of host. But He is also grieved when we let *"that which cometh upon us daily"* make a difference in our love. He said: *And blessed is he, whosoever shall not be offended in me.* Matthew 11:6

In Deuteronomy 13:3, 4, He told the people of Israel to expect trials. *"…for the LORD your God proveth you, to know whether ye love the LORD your God with all your heart and with all your soul. Ye shall walk after the LORD your God, and fear him, and keep his commandments, and obey his voice, and ye shall serve him, and cleave unto him."*

Our problems - whether "911" or "uh-oh" moments – are a chance for us to do our best, a chance for us to prove our love. Giving mankind his own will was risky for Him and risky for those He created, but it was the only way God's purpose could be brought about.

God asks for my trust: He has told me: *"…but he that endureth to the end shall be saved."* Matthew 10:22 *"Thou shalt be recompensed…"* Luke 14:14 Jesus is the *"Author and finisher of my faith…."* Hebrews 12:2 *"Many are the afflictions of the righteous: but the LORD delivereth him out of them all.* Psalm 34:19

His beloved say: *"Though He slay me, yet will I serve him. The Lord giveth* (and oh how He has given) *and the Lord taketh away. Blessed be the name of the Lord." "Shall I receive good at the hand of God, and shall we not receive evil?" "In my flesh I shall see God."*

Am I serving Him just for the loaves and the fishes -- for all the wonderful benefits that accompany salvation and all the good things I receive at the hand of God. Am I going to be faithful, no matter what? He wants my allegiance, my worship, my love, my trust. Let's not miss a chance to prove our love to Him.

Therefore I take pleasure in infirmities, in reproaches, in necessities, in persecutions, in distresses for Christ's sake: for when I am weak, then am I strong. 2 Corinthians 12:10

Although the fig tree shall not blossom, neither shall fruit be in the vines; the labour of the olive shall fail, and the fields shall yield no meat; the flock shall be cut off from the fold, and there shall be no herd in the stalls: Yet I will rejoice in the LORD, I will joy in the God of my salvation. The LORD God is my strength…. Habakkuk 3: 17-19

Satan: Today I am certainly not serving God for nought - But I hope that I would….

Recommended Resources

Carlson, Richard. Don't Sweat the Small Stuff, and It's All Small Stuff: Simple Ways to Keep the Little Things from Taking Over Your Life. New York: Hyperion Books, 1997. Print.

Williams, Mike. Message: "Build-Plant-Marry-Beget." Because of the Times. 2011. DVD or CD of message. The Pentecostals of Alexandria (thepentecostals.org)

Artist Laura Story Song: *Blessings,*
https://www.youtube.com/watch?v=1CSVqHcdhXQ

That Which Cometh Upon Me Daily Workbook as a PDF file is available on request to mwolfe242@aol.com ($5.00)

That Which Cometh Upon Me Daily PowerPoint available on request to mwolfe242@aol. com, no charge.

LIFE APPLICATION

1. Consider your own life—your fiery trials and your aggravations.

a. List:

1) Tragedies, Serious Sickness, Trauma, and True Hardships

2) Chronic Aggravations of Life/Frustrations

b. Which affects you the most—the true tragedies or the constant frustrations?

c. Which has had a lasting effect?

d. Which do you deal with the best?

e. What causes you to get "bent out of shape"? What really angers you?

2. We can be either a thermostat, and help control the "temperatures" around us, or a thermometer and react with every wind that blows. Consider the following people from Bible and the times when they affected the climate around them and/or the times when they let the climate affect them.

Samson—Judges 13-16

Moses—Exodus 14, Numbers 20:8-12, Psalm 106:33

David—1 Samuel 30:6, 2 Samuel 11

Peter—Matthew 26:69-74

3. Look closely at your concept of God. Is your relationship reciprocal? Or is it all entitlement from your perspective? Do you ask God just what you would like for Him to do for you—or do you ask what He would want you to do for Him?

NOTES:

With all my problems:

If today I were blind, I would be so happy to receive my sight.

If I were crippled, I would be ecstatic to be able to walk again.

If I were threatened, in danger for my life, kidnapped, a hostage, I would be so joyous to be rescued.

If I were hungry, I would be so thankful for provision of food.

If I were cold or hot, exposed to the elements, I would be so glad to have shelter, warmth.

If I had the knowledge that I or a loved one had a terminal illness, I would be thrilled for restored health.

If one of my loved ones were to die, I would be ecstatic to have them restored

But today, I can see. I can hear. My loved ones are alive, I am not hungry, cold, destitute. I am not endangered, I am in good health.

I will rejoice!

DON'T BLAME GOD

"And blessed is he, whosoever shall not be offended in me."

John the Baptist knew the power of Jesus.

> *Now when John had heard in the prison the works of Christ, he sent two of his disciples, And said unto him, Art thou he that should come, or do we look for another? Jesus answered and said unto them, Go and shew John again those things which ye do hear and see: The blind receive their sight, and the lame walk, the lepers are cleansed, and the deaf hear, the dead are raised up, and the poor have the gospel preached to them. And blessed is he, whosoever shall not be offended in me.* Matthew 11:2-6

Earlier in his ministry John had announced,

> *"There cometh one mightier than I after me, the latchet of whose shoes I am not worthy to stoop down and unloose."* Mark 1:7 He was ready to turn His ministry over to Jesus: *"He must increase, I must decrease."*

Now John is hurting, wounded, twisting on the question marks in his life. "Art thou he that should come? or look we for another?" Jesus' answer to John's disciples was, *Jesus answered and said unto them, Go and shew John again those things which ye do hear and see: The blind receive their sight, and the lame walk, the lepers are cleansed, and the deaf hear, the dead are raised up, and the poor have the gospel reached to them. And blessed is he, whosoever shall not be offended in me.* Matthew 11:4-6

John could easily have become offended by these miracles. Others were getting miraculous deliverances, phenomenal healings and he could have thought, "Here I am rotting in jail." And he was the one about whom Jesus said, "None greater." *Verily I say unto you, Among them that are born of women there hath not risen a greater than John the Baptist...* Matthew 11:11. Now John is told: "*...blessed is he, whosoever shall not be offended in me.*" In other words, "John, don't get hurt feelings toward God. Don't blame God. Don't get offended by miracles."

We all know the story of Job's troubles.

Then Job arose, and rent his mantle, and shaved his head, and fell down upon the ground, and worshipped, And said, Naked came I out of my mother's womb, and naked shall I return thither: the LORD gave, and the LORD hath taken away; blessed be the name of the LORD. In all this Job sinned not, nor charged God foolishly. Job 1:20-22

Job's reactions were very similar to what ours would have been: He prayed to die. "I wish I'd never been born." "What I have feared has come upon me." "My soul is weary." The book says he was perfect and upright, that he feared God and eschewed evil. And Job made it clear that he would have understood his troubles if he had not done what was right. *Doth not he see my ways, and count all my steps? If I have walked with vanity, or if my foot hath hasted to deceit; Let me be weighed in an even balance that God may know mine integrity. If my step hath turned out of the way, and mine heart walked after mine eyes, and if any blot hath cleaved to mine hands;....If mine heart have been deceived by a woman, or if I have laid wait at my neighbour's door.... If I did despise the cause of my manservant or of my maidservant, when they contended with me; If I have withheld the poor from their desire, or have caused the eyes of the widow to fail; ...or have eaten my morsel myself alone, and the fatherless hath not eaten thereof;… If I have seen any perish for want of clothing, or any poor without covering; …If I have lifted up my hand against the fatherless, when I saw my help in the gate…. If I rejoice at the destruction of him that hated me, or lifted up myself when evil found him: Neither have I suffered my mouth to sin by wishing a curse to his soul.* (From Job 31)

But he did not charge God foolishly. *"In all this Job sinned not, nor charged God foolishly."* Perhaps he was hurt, even a little offended at God; one can see clearly that he was feeling forsaken, let down, abandoned, but not blaming God.

Perhaps his feelings were similar to that of a dear friend of mine with recurrent breast cancer which eventually was terminal. She was faithfully doing the work of God. She told me, "I feel like a child that had been thrown up into the air by her father and then allowed to fall to the ground."

It is okay to ask questions. It is okay even to express, "I don't understand." But do not blame God. Have you ever been blamed for something you did not do, blamed for something you could not help? Have you been berated for something that you did for someone (for their good)? Then you know, it is very hurtful to be "charged foolishly."

Troublesome times will come. *"Man is of few days and full of trouble."* It is human nature to question, "My God, why?" We are in very good company when we do so.

DAVID: *I will say unto God my rock, Why hast thou forgotten me? why go I mourning because of the oppression of the enemy?* Psalm 42:9
LORD, why castest thou off my soul? why hidest thou thy face from me? I am afflicted and ready to die from my youth up: while I suffer thy terrors I am distracted. Psalm 88:14,15

SOLOMON: *Then said I in my heart, As it happeneth to the fool, so it happeneth even to me; and why was I then more wise? Then I said in my heart, that this also is vanity.* Ecclesiastes 2:15

JEREMIAH: *Why is my pain perpetual, and my wound incurable, which refuseth to be healed? wilt thou be altogether unto me as a liar, and as waters that fail?* Jeremiah 15:18

HABAKKUK: *O LORD, how long shall I cry, and thou wilt not hear! even cry out unto thee of violence, and thou wilt not save! Why dost thou shew me iniquity, and cause me to behold grievance? for spoiling and violence are before me: and there are that raise up strife and contention.* Habakkuk 1:2-3

THE MARTYRS IN REVELATIONS: *And when he had opened the fifth seal, I saw under the altar the souls of them that were slain for the word of God, and for the testimony which they held: And they cried with a loud voice, saying, How long, O Lord, holy and true, dost thou not judge and avenge our blood on them that dwell on the earth?* Revelations 6:9-10

EVEN JESUS: *And about the ninth hour Jesus cried with a loud voice, saying, Eli, Eli, lama sabachthani? that is to say, My God, my God, why hast thou forsaken me?* Matthew 27:46

We will often have unanswered questions, but it is important that we not "charge God foolishly."

HOW DO WE CHARGE GOOD WRONGLY?

One way we can blame/charge God foolishly is to think everything bad that comes our way is a God thing, "God did this to me, it is God's fault."

Discussion: Have you ever wondered why we call the most devastating events "acts of God"? Some things are part of life, written in the very laws of nature. That's the way it is. We can count on it! The tide comes in; the tide goes out. There are valleys and mountains. Night follows day. In every life there is sunshine and there is rain. Winter follows summer; old age follows youth. The sun came up this morning and will set tonight. Whatever seed I plant will be what comes up. If I plant beans, no matter how much I fast and pray, corn is not going to come up. *Be not deceived; God is not mocked: for whatsoever a man soweth, that shall he also reap*…Galatians 6:7-8

The laws of God are inescapable, inevitable, written in the very fabric of life. If I defy gravity, I will smash! One will get old - no matter how faithful. Old age is a tragedy – but it happens to all. And it is appointed unto men to die. Also time and chance happen to all: *I returned, and saw under the sun, that the race is not to the swift, nor the battle to the strong, neither yet bread to the wise, nor yet riches to men of understanding, nor yet favour to men of skill; but time and chance happeneth to them all.* Ecclesiastes 9:11

God did not "do it" to me. Nature did. Life did. Often life is not fair. The good die young. Princes walk, beggars ride. *(I have seen servants upon horses, and princes walking as servants upon the earth.* Ecclesiastes 10:7) I get bad things I do not deserve. I also get a lot of good things I do not deserve. Peter expressed it this way: "... *knowing that the same afflictions are accomplished in your brethren that are in the world.*" 1 Peter 5:9

We sometimes will feel like Simple Simon: "Why does everything happen to me, I'm always in some kind of jam. I'm no good at all, no wonder they call me simple, I guess I am."

Life is not fair: Sometimes the good will die young. Again, sometimes I get bad things I don't deserve. Sometimes I get good things I don't deserve.

JOB: *And said, Naked came I out of my mother's womb, and naked shall I return thither: the LORD gave, and the LORD hath taken away; blessed be the name of the LORD.* Job 1:21 … *What? shall we receive good at the hand of God, and shall we not receive evil? In all this did not Job sin with his lips.* Job 2:10

In Job 8:5-6, Job's "comforter," Bildad, told Job: *If thou wouldest seek unto God betimes, and make thy supplication to the Almighty; If thou wert pure and upright; surely now he would awake for thee, and make the habitation of thy righteousness prosperous.*

God said to Eliphaz about Job's friends' words: *My wrath is kindled against thee, and against thy two friends: for ye have not spoken of me the thing that is right, as my servant Job hath.* Job 42:7

Jesus made it clear: *"(Your Father which is in heaven) maketh his sun to rise on the evil and on the good, and sendeth rain on the just and on the unjust."* Matthew 5:45

Another way we can blame/charge God foolishly is to feel that bad things that happen are God's punishment for something we did.

First of all, God is not malicious, vindictive. God does not berate, strike in anger. God is slow to anger as witnessed and testified throughout the Bible - by Nehemiah, Jonah, David, Joel, Nahum, and many others.

I once had to take my grandson to a day care on my way to work. For some reason he thought it was because of something he did and kept crying, "Mammaw, I'm sorry." (He was "charging me foolishly.")

If thou, LORD, shouldest mark iniquities, O Lord, who shall stand? But there is forgiveness with thee, that thou mayest be feared.

Psalm 130:3 to 4

...But thou art a God ready to pardon, gracious and merciful, slow to anger, and of great kindness, and forsookest them not. Nehemiah 9:17

The LORD is merciful and gracious, slow to anger, and plenteous in mercy. He will not always chide: neither will he keep his anger for ever. He hath not dealt with us after our sins; nor rewarded us according to our iniquities. Psalm 103:8-10

The LORD is gracious, and full of compassion; slow to anger, and of great mercy. The LORD is good to all: and his tender mercies are over all his works. Psalm 145:8-9

For God sent not his Son into the world to condemn the world; but that the world through him might be saved. John 3:17

God convicts and corrects. He encourages and edifies. Sometimes God will chastise but it will always be for our good, never to hurt or destroy.

Is it condemnation or conviction? We can judge if our thoughts regarding this are from God or from Satan.

Satan: He is: *"... the accuser of our brethren.... which accused them before our God day and night."* Revelations 12:10. He condemns. He reminds us of our failures he taunts, "You deserve this." We will have a sense of guilt, hopelessness. "You blew it - you are washed up."

Jesus: He is "the intercessor" Who *"ever liveth to make intercession"* Hebrews 7:25 *"And the Lord said, Simon, Simon, behold, Satan hath desired to have you, that he may sift you as wheat: But I have prayed for thee, that thy faith fail not...* Luke 22:31

Even when we brought some of our problems on ourselves, He'll help us overcome. *"Wherefore he is able also to save them to the uttermost that come unto God by him, seeing he ever liveth to make intercession for them."* Hebrews 7:25. He offers hope instead of hopelessness! "You can do better. I'll help you fix it." *"Neither do I condemn thee, go and sin no more."*

Who is a God like unto thee, that pardoneth iniquity, and passeth by the transgression of the remnant of his heritage? he retaineth not his anger for ever, because he delighteth in mercy. Micah 7:18

Thirdly, we can falsely blame God and charge God that if He would, He could prevent this from happening, He could spare me.

There are some things God cannot do because He limits Himself. There are things God has delegated... turned over to someone else. He has given man free will and dominion.

And God said, Let us make man in our image, after our likeness: and let them have dominion over the fish of the sea, and over the fowl of the air, and over the cattle, and over all the earth, and over every creeping thing that creepeth upon the earth. Genesis 1:26

For thou hast made him a little lower than the angels, and hast crowned him with glory and honour. Thou madest him to have dominion over the works of thy hands; thou hast put all things under his feet: All sheep and oxen, yea, and the beasts of the field; The fowl of the air, and the fish of the sea, and whatsoever passeth through the paths of the seas. Psalm 8:5-8

What man does with this dominion often makes God very sad. Violence and crimes grieve God. *Justice is turned back, and righteousness stands afar off; for truth is fallen in the street, and equity cannot enter. So truth fails, and he who departs from evil makes himself a prey. Then the LORD saw it, and it displeased Him that there was no justice. He saw that there was no man, and wondered that there was no intercessor; therefore His own arm brought salvation for Him; and His own righteousness, it sustained Him.* Isaiah 59:14-15

The Lord saw it and it displeased Him! He has delegated the responsibility of doing some things to mankind. We ask, "Why doesn't God act?" He is "wondering" that we do not do something against injustice (v.15).

Why doesn't God do something?
Why doesn't He intervene?"
He did. It was epic.
Remember Calvary?
That was Him - doing something!
(Tweet from Facebook)

Righteousness will prevail, truth shall triumph in the end. *"Many are the afflictions of the righteous, but God delivered out of them all."* Psalm 34:19. You shall be recompensed. There is payday someday. *"Behold, the righteous shall be recompensed in the earth:* Proverbs 11:31. The books will be balanced, however, maybe not today.

Another friend of Job, Eliphaz, said: *"Remember, I pray thee, who ever perished, being innocent? or where were the righteous cut off?* Job 4:7 Well, Eliphaz, there were a few before Job and a few after Job, to name just a few: Abel, Naboth, Isaiah, John the Baptist, 11 of the 12 apostles, etc., etc.

The final result will be victory – but for a time, sometimes, "there is no justice."

Another limit: God limits Himself for our ultimate good.

If a son asked for bread, will He give a stone...Or what man is there of you, whom if his son ask bread, will he give him a stone? Or if he ask a fish, will he give him a serpent? If ye then, being evil, know how to give good gifts unto your children, how much more shall your Father which is in heaven give good things to them that ask him? Matthew 7:9-11

Consider this: Even if a child asks for a stone to eat, a loving father will not give him a stone, but will give him bread. If a toddler begs for a knife, a loving father will not give it to him no matter how distressed he becomes.

Discussion: Have you ever prayed for something fervently and never received your answer, then later down the road realized how bad that would have been for you – or how much better another answer was?

> *Ye ask, and receive not, because ye ask amiss, that ye may consume it upon your lusts.* James 4:*3*
>
> *And this is the confidence that we have in him, that, if we ask any thing according to his will, he heareth us: And if we know that he hear us, whatsoever we ask, we know that we have the petitions that we desired of him.* I John 5:14-15
>
> *Wherefore let them that suffer according to the will of God commit the keeping of their souls to him in well doing, as unto a faithful Creator.* 1 Peter 4:19

A faithful man of God I knew suffered serious health problems, cancer, amputation of leg, and many other ills. He told of his questioning God, asking for understanding of why his prayers for healing had not been answered. The Spirit spoke to him saying, "You have prayed prayers that superseded your prayers for healing."

We often have many prayers on the altars of our lives: Prayers for salvation for us and our loved ones, prayers for our financial needs (perhaps for a particular job), prayers for companionship, love. Sometimes these prayers are contradictory. We can be praying for opposites. Joseph's prayers for delivery from the pit would have been contrary to his dreams for his family.

Last but not least: Don't blame/charge God foolishly that he does not care.

"...and he was in the hinder part of the ship, asleep on a pillow: and they awake him, and say unto him, Master, carest thou not that we perish? Mark 4:38

For I said in my haste, I am cut off from before thine eyes: nevertheless thou heardest the voice of my supplications when I cried unto thee. O love the LORD, *all ye his saints: for the* LORD *preserveth the faithful, and plentifully rewardeth the proud doer. Be of good courage, and he shall strengthen your heart, all ye that hope in the* LORD. Psalm 31:22-24

But Zion said, The LORD *hath forsaken me, and my Lord hath forgotten me. Can a woman forget her sucking child, that she should not have compassion on the son of her womb? yea, they may forget, yet will I not forget thee. Behold, I have graven thee upon the palms of my hands; thy walls are continually before me.* Isaiah 49:14-16

This is the probably the most reprehensible thing we can think about our Heavenly Father who loves us so. We have so many assurances from His word that He grieves with us, that He knows, He sees, He cares.

When thou passest through the waters, I will be with thee; and through the rivers, they shall not overflow thee: when thou walkest through the fire, thou shalt not be burned; neither shall the flame kindle upon thee. For I am the LORD *thy God, the Holy One of Israel, thy Saviour: I gave Egypt for thy ransom, Ethiopia and Seba for thee. Since thou wast precious in my sight, thou hast been honourable, and I have loved thee: therefore will I give men for thee, and people for thy life. Fear not: for I am with thee: I will bring thy seed from the east, and gather thee from the west;* Isaiah 43:2-5

Fear thou not; for I am with thee: be not dismayed; for I am thy God: I will strengthen thee; yea, I will help thee; yea, I will uphold thee with the right hand of my righteousness. Isaiah 41:10

Casting all your care upon him; for he careth for you. 1 Peter 5:7

Cast not away therefore your confidence, which hath great recompence of reward. For ye have need of patience, that, after ye have done the will of God, ye might receive the promise. For yet a little while, and he that shall come will come, and will not tarry. Hebrews 10:35-37

Behold, we count them happy which endure. Ye have heard of the patience of Job, and have seen the end of the Lord; that the Lord is very pitiful, and of tender mercy. James 5:11

Knowing this, that the trying of your faith worketh patience. But let patience have her perfect work, that ye may be perfect and entire, wanting nothing. James 1:3-4

Blessed is the man that endureth temptation: for when he is tried, he shall receive the crown of life, which the Lord hath promised to them that love him. James 1:12

Wherein ye greatly rejoice, though now for a season, if need be, ye are in heaviness through manifold temptations: That the trial of your faith, being much more precious than of gold that perisheth, though it be tried with fire, might be found unto praise and honour and glory at the appearing of Jesus Christ: Whom having not seen, ye love; in whom, though now ye see him not, yet believing, ye rejoice with joy unspeakable and full of glory: Receiving the end of your faith, even the salvation of your souls. 1 Peter 1:6-9

What time I am afraid, I will trust in thee. In God I will praise his word, in God I have put my trust; I will not fear what flesh can do unto me. Psalm 56:3-4

For I know that my redeemer liveth, and that he shall stand at the latter day upon the earth: And though after my skin worms destroy this body, yet in my flesh shall I see God: Job 19:25-26

These things I have spoken unto you, that in me ye might have peace. In the world ye shall have tribulation: but be of good cheer; I have overcome the world. John 16:33

He knows, He sees, He cares. Oh, how He loves you and me. Our righteousness, our salvation is His ultimate purpose. *For I know the thoughts that I think toward you, saith the LORD, thoughts of peace, and not of evil, to give you an expected end.* Jeremiah 29:11

The Eternal Goodness

Within the maddening maze of things,
When tossed by storm and flood,
To one fixed trust my spirit clings;
I know that God is good!
I know not what the future hath
Of marvel or surprise,
Assured alone that life and death
His mercy underlies
No offering of my own I have,
Nor works my faith to prove;
I can but give the gifts He gave,
And plead His love for love.
And so beside the silent sea
I wait the muffled oar;
No harm from Him can come to me
On ocean or on shore.
I know not where His islands lift
Their fronded palms in air;
I only know I cannot drift
Beyond His love and care.

Extracted from "The Eternal Goodness"
written in 1867 by John Greenleaf Whittier

Recommended Resources
Dobson, James. When God Doesn't Make Sense. Carol Stream, Illinois: Tyndale House Publishers, 1993. Print.
Lucado, Max. In the Eye of the Storm. Nashville, Tennessee: Thomas Nelson, 1997 Print

Don't Blame God Workbook as a PDF file is available on request to mwolfe242@aol.com ($5.00)
Don't Blame God PowerPoint available on request to mwolfe242@aol. com, no charge.

LIFE APPLICATION

1. Matthew 11:6 says, "And blessed is he, whosoever shall not be offended in me." What does it mean to be offended in God?

2. Despite all of Job's suffering, the Bible states that "In all this Job sinned not, nor charged God foolishly" (Job 1:22). Consider the full meaning behind this scripture. Did Job have questions for God? Was he confused? What did he say that showed he was very disheartened or even depressed? 3. What did Job say that lets us know he still trusted God? (Job 1:21, 2:10, 19:26) 4. Read 1 Timothy 6:5. Do you see a parallel in the thinking of many Christians today that trouble and hardships mean that one is out of the will of God or that one has sinned?

5. List specific examples of how the mindset portrayed in 1

Timothy 6:5 is reflected in the statements made by Job's friends.

6. What statements did Jesus make that directly refute or challenge this belief?

7. Find scriptures asserting that God is "slow to anger," and write them below.

8. See how many scriptures you can find asserting His mercy endureth (His mercy is everlasting).

9. Review the lesson and the many scriptures that reassure us of His care. Write out the scriptures that speak forcibly to your heart, and commit them to memory.

NOTES:

BOUND BY BRUISES

"He hath sent me...to set at liberty them that are bruised."

> *And he came to Nazareth, where he had been brought up: and, as his custom was, he went into the synagogue on the sabbath day, and stood up for to read. And there was delivered unto him the book of the prophet Esaias. And when he had opened the book, he found the place where it was written, The Spirit of the Lord is upon me, because he hath anointed me to preach the gospel to the poor; he hath sent me to heal the brokenhearted, to preach deliverance to the captives, and recovering of sight to the blind, to set at liberty them that are bruised, To preach the acceptable year of the Lord.* Luke 4:16-19

Jesus continued in verse 21: *"This day is this scripture fulfilled in your ears."* Jesus came to earth in part to *"set at liberty them that are bruised."* And if you fit any of these categories: He is here, *"as his custom is"* (when two or three are gathered in His name), *"to heal the brokenhearted, preach deliverance to the captives, recovering of sight to the blind," and to "set at liberty them that are bruised."* You are in the right place at the right time.

This passage that Jesus chose to read that day was from Isaiah 61:1. The translation from the Hebrew of this Old Testament passage was, *The Spirit of the Lord GOD is upon me; because the LORD hath anointed me to preach good tidings unto the meek; he hath sent me to bind up the brokenhearted, to proclaim liberty to the captives, and the opening of the prison to them that are bound.* Isaiah 61:1

Where the verse in Isaiah reads *"opening of prison to them that are bound,"* the one in Luke is phrased, *"to set at liberty the bruised."* Rather than "healing the bruised," it is somewhat cryptically written as *"opening the prison of the bound and setting at liberty the bruised."* We can take from this that we can be bound by our bruises, that we need freedom from that bondage, and that He is come to set us at liberty "*this day.*"

All of us have been bruised by life. Our bruises are tangible, visible evidence that we have been hurt. Bruises are obvious; bruises are marked. We can prove that something happened. Sometimes we cannot even remember where we got the bruise – but we know we were hurt. Bruises can come from a direct assault, accidental or intentional; but they can also be caused by constant pricks, falls, or running headlong into something.

Bruises are not always the result of someone else's carelessness or intent to harm; sometimes they are self-inflicted. In fact, many bruises are our own fault --- and a reminder of our falls and our own clumsiness.

In the physical we are often bound by our bruises. Once we are hurt attempting something, we will not attempt that again soon. We fall --- and then subsequently we have a fear of climbing.

Nothing binds our spirit like hurt feelings, bruises to our emotions or our self-image. We are tempted to draw into a shell, not to attempt again. "I won't witness, I got hurt one time, I have a bruise to remind me," (even though I may have witnessed many times without getting hurt). "I won't trust, I got hurt doing that." "I won't love unconditionally; I got hurt."

You are not going to stub your toe unless you are trying to go somewhere. You will not fall unless you are reaching for heights. One does not usually fall out of their rocking chair. You will not make mistakes unless you are attempting something. It is true: *Ships are safe in harbor - but that's not what ships are for.* The worst thing for a bruised limb is immobilization. The limb becomes weaker and atrophied.

Some people wear bruises like medals. They say, "I bruise so easily," and then will show them to anyone that will commiserate. Sometimes pressing a bruise brings satisfaction, feeling the hurt that brings. We can do that with emotional hurts as well, "Do you know how this one or that one hurt me?"

But that is not God's will for us; He wants "to set at liberty them that are bruised." Why do we hold on to our bruises? *"Is there no balm in Gilead? Is there no physician there? Why then is not health of the daughter of my people recovered?* Jeremiah 8:22

There is a healing balm; there is a doctor in the house! Today, this day, this scripture can be fulfilled in your life.

Then they cry unto the LORD in their trouble, and he saveth them out of their distresses. He sent his word, and healed them, and delivered them from their destructions. Psalms 107:19-20

Sometimes past hurts cause us to be hurt more by things that should not hurt at all. These past hurts make us more sensitive, more vulnerable to injury.

I recall an incident when I was a teenager in high school. One day in the usual pandemonium in the hallways between classes, I was rushing along with everyone else. Suddenly, right in my ear, came a bloodcurdling scream. One would have thought someone had been stabbed or mortally injured. All eyes turned on me as the perpetrator. In my hurry, I had brushed by a teacher, jostling her. The contact was not rough --- but the pain was bad. Ms. Wilson's arm had been broken and was in a cast. When she was touched, her hurt was magnified, her pain way out of proportion to the incident. Her reaction was understandable --- she already had been hurt, and now she was experiencing again the trauma of a broken arm. I didn't break her arm, but it felt like it to her because her injury had not healed.

Our past emotional hurts if left unhealed cause us to be hurt by trivial things. We react! We have a "sore spot." Our reactions are tinted by our experiences; *"For now we see through a glass darkly,"* a glass that is foggy because of past incidents. My response in any given situation is magnified by things that have happened to me. We say, someone "stepped on my toes," or "pulled my chain," or that "hit a sore spot."

Every one of us has been bruised by life. We all have had hard knocks and reverses, constant pricks and direct assaults, and whether it is intentional or from carelessness, we hurt. We may say, "Sticks and stones may break my bones - but words will never hurt me," but words can and do hurt.

In his book, Words that Hurt, Words that Heal, Rabbi Telushkin made the following statement: "Unless you or someone dear to you has been the victim of terrible physical violence, chances are the worst pains you have suffered in life have come from words used cruelly – from ego-destroying criticism, excessive anger, sarcasm, public and private humiliation, hurtful nicknames, betrayal of secrets, rumors and malicious gossip" *(Words That Hurt, Words That Heal: How to Choose Words Wisely and Well,* Joseph Telushkin, p. xviii).

Perhaps intended to hurt, perhaps not, the hurt is just the same. We can feel battered, bruised in spirit, and pushed around by life. Some of us may have been knocked off our feet or slammed to the floor --- by a mere slip of the tongue. Maybe today you are "punch drunk." Some of us have bruises that we don't even know how we got them. We just know we have been hurt, crippled, broken emotionally. Some have bruises that I cannot relate to, bruises that I cannot see, bruises that have never been revealed to anyone, but they are nevertheless real. You may say to me: "You just don't know!"

However, we do know that Jesus is no stranger to bruises. We cannot say to Him, "You've never been there." He has been there and He has not forgotten, nor will He ever forget what it was to be there. Although your friends or family may not be able to empathize and relate, He can.

He was rejected and abused. *He was despised and rejected of men, a man of sorrows, and acquainted with grief. He was despised and we esteemed him not. He hath borne our griefs and carried our sorrows yet we did esteem him stricken, smitten of God and afflicted…* Isaiah 53:3-4

He was oppressed and afflicted. *"For we have not an high priest which cannot be touched with the feeling of our infirmities; but was in all points tempted like as we are, yet without sin."* Hebrews 4:15. Note: "*In all points tempted like as we are*" --- evidently there were many unrecorded experiences of suffering about which we were not told.

His friends in Nazareth said, *"He is beside himself."* (Mark 3:21) We know His brothers did not believe in Him, and even told Him to go away. (John 7:1-7) And the scribes that came down from Jerusalem said, *"He hath Beelzebub, and by the prince of the devils casteth he out devils."* (Mark 3:22) He was betrayed by one friend and companion for an insultingly small sum. Another "best friend" denied, cursed, and said, "I don't even know him."

He was forsaken by all (Mark 14:50), evidently even the beloved John.

In fact, Isaiah 53 says *"He was wounded for my transgressions, he was bruised for my iniquity."* Not only was He wounded for my transgressions, he is also wounded by my transgressions. My neglect of Him, my lack of reciprocation of His love, my lack of response, my carelessness, my wrongs have bruised Him. Hebrews 6:6 tells that *"If they shall fall away...they crucify to themselves the Son of God afresh, and put him to an open shame."*

But this bruised One came to set at liberty them that are bruised...to bind up the brokenhearted.

In any given trauma, how we react is the most important thing! The worst scenario we endure is only as bad as its lasting effect on us. Even in the physical, the important thing is not how bad we have been hurt, but whether we can heal completely, whether we can get over it. Surgery would be unspeakable torture - but if we are anesthetized, if we do not recall, if we recover, the outcome is health.

In the emotional realm, it is not what has happened, but whether we can be whole again, can we forget.

We sometimes say, "I forgave, but I can't forget!" But we can forget! The same God who daily washes all the sands on the seashores of the worlds can wash the memories from the mind! (If, Amy Carmichael)

In Man's Search for Meaning, Viktor E. Frankl, a survivor of a concentration camp during World War II, told of his incarceration, of unspeakable atrocities, of humiliation, and of seeing his loved ones killed. He came to this conclusion: "Everything can be taken from a man but ... the last of the human freedoms -- to choose one's attitude in any given set of circumstances, to choose one's own way" (Frankl, Viktor E., Man's Search for Meaning, Washington Square Press, Simon and Schuster, New York, 1963).

We often say things like, "You made me angry" or "They made me nervous." The honest thing to say would be "I got angry" or "I got nervous." No one can "make me" act in any way. We can decide, "No man's conduct shall determine mine!" Bitterness cannot be inflicted or imposed on us. Bitterness is not what someone does to me. Bitterness is something I choose.

> "Your greatest enemy is not betrayal from others,
> but bitterness toward those who betray you."

Discussion:

- What I am, plus what I think, equals what I become.
- My reaction to the problem ends up the problem.
- It is not what happens TO me but what happens IN me.

There were two brilliant brothers in our times, with the same father, the same mother; raised together with the same opportunities. One went to Harvard, the other to Columbia University. One brother, Ted, with bitterness and animosity took lives of innocent people who were complete strangers to him. He was the Unabomber. The other brother, David, although extremely reluctant to expose one he was convinced was guilty (even for a reward of $1,000,000) ultimately turned his brother in with much anguish but with determination to do the right thing.

There were two young men orphaned by the Oklahoma City bombing. One young man, Robbie, bought into the victim mentality. By the age of 23, he had turned to alcohol, cocaine, and ended up in prison. Another young man, Tim Hearn, gave up a football college scholarship to take care of his brothers and sisters, a noble, selfless hero.

The same sun that hardens clay will melt wax! Adversities that make one man a criminal will make another a prince. Two birds, the vulture and the hummingbird, traverse the same terrain. One sees carnage, rotting, smelly dead meat. The other sees beautiful little flowers, fragrant, colorful beauty. Traversing the same territory, each one finds what he is looking for. If we look for the evils of our situation, no matter how blessed we are, we can find. If we look for good in our situation, no matter how much trouble we are in, we can find.

When we face hurt in our lives, we have two choices: We can cast all our cares upon Him and let Him bind up our broken hearts. We can run to Him with our hurts, for He reacts "as a father pitieth his children," He will take us in His arms and soothe all hurts. He will let us know that everything is going to be all right. *"And because ye are sons, God hath sent forth the Spirit of his Son into your hearts, crying, Abba, Father."* Galatians 4:6 *Men groan from out of the city, and the soul of the wounded crieth out: yet God layeth not folly to them.* (or God doth not regard it as foolish). Job 24:12

OR We can nurse our hurts and get satisfaction in pressing on bruises. We can 'lick our wounds,' 'count our booboos,' or bang our head against the wall. We can let our wounds fester, as we twist and turn on the hooks of question marks in our lives. This opens up our lives for a *"root of bitterness"* whereby *"many will be defiled"* Hebrews 12:15

Our reactions, our attitudes, are our choice. We can choose healing. *Is there no balm in Gilead; is there no physician there? why then is not the health of the daughter of my people recovered?* Jeremiah 8:22

Why are you holding on to your bruises? There is a physician with compassion to pick you up out of the ditch, to bind up your wounds, and to take care of you.

Luke 13:34 "... *how often would I have gathered thy children together, as a hen doth gather her brood under her wings, and ye would not!"*

Matthew 11:28 "*Come unto me, all ye that labour and are heavy laden, and I will give you rest.*"

Luke 4:18, 21 *"The spirit of the Lord is upon me, Because he hath anointed me to preach the Gospel to the poor; he hath sent me to heal the brokenhearted, to preach deliverance to the captives and recovering of the sight to the blind, to set at liberty them that are bruised [. . .] this day is this scripture fulfilled [. . .]"*

Isaiah 61:1 *The Spirit of the Lord GOD is upon me… V.3 To appoint unto them that mourn in Zion, to give unto them beauty for ashes, the oil of joy for mourning, the garment of praise for the spirit of heaviness; that they might be called trees of righteousness, the planting of the LORD, that he might be glorified.*

"What a friend we have in Jesus... in His arms He'll take and shield thee. Thou wilt find a solace there."

Charles C. Converse, 1868, (Public Domain)

One ship sails east, and another drives west
With the selfsame winds that blow
Tis the set of the sails and not the gales
Which tells us the way to go

Like the winds of the sea are the ways of Fate.
As we voyage along through life
Tis the set of a soul that decides its goal
And not the calm or the strife.

ELLA WHEELER WILCOX, American writer, poet and journalist (1850 - 1919)

Recommended Resources:
Bound By Bruises Workbook as a PDF file is available on request to mwolfe242@aol.com ($5.00)
Bound by Bruises PowerPoint is available on request to mwolfe242@aol. com, no charge.

LIFE APPLICATION

1. Think of bruises you have received in life. Discuss how these bruises have affected/bound you.

2. Discuss how these bruises cause you to be more sensitive in certain areas of your life.

3. How many scriptures can you find that let you know He wants you to be healed?

4. Read Isaiah 53. Make a list of the specific ways Jesus fulfilled these prophecies.

5. What particular hurts did He endure that you can relate to?
6. In what ways have you hurt Him?

NOTES:

TRIAL OF YOUR FAITH

... I have prayed for thee, that thy faith fail not

> *Let us draw near with a true heart in full assurance of faith, having our hearts sprinkled from an evil conscience, and our bodies washed with pure water. Let us hold fast the profession of our faith without wavering; (for he is faithful that promised);* Hebrews 10:22-23

We are all familiar with assaults on our faith, sometimes even severe crises of faith. We are sometimes blind sided with revelations that someone in whom we had great confidence lost their faith. Something threw them! Then we are reminded of the many that are faithful against all the odds.

That the trial of your faith, being much more precious than of gold that perisheth, though it be tried with fire, might be found unto praise and honour and glory at the appearing of Jesus Christ. 1 Peter 1:7

Sometimes we feel like crying out with our Lord: *Nevertheless when the Son of man cometh, shall he find faith on the earth?* Luke 18:8 What is important for you and for me is not the road we have traveled to get here, but where we are. It is not what has happened to me that is decisive but what has happened <u>in</u> me. When He comes will He find faith... in ME?

> *And the Lord said, Simon, Simon, behold, Satan hath desired to have you, that he may sift you as wheat: But I have prayed for thee, that thy faith fail not: and when thou art converted, strengthen thy brethren.* Luke 22:31-32

Today we have good news and bad news. The bad news

is Satan hath desired to sift you as wheat. He wants to make mincemeat - of your resolve, your consecration, your revelation. The good news is "Someone is praying for you." Satan has desired to sift ... Jesus has prayed for you. You are part of an eternal triangle. You, Satan, and Jesus. On the one hand: Satan desires to sift you as wheat. On the other hand: Jesus is praying for you.

How comforting I find it to have many prayer warriors who care about me - and my faith: My pastor, my church, my godly friends. What a treasure it is in 'trials of faith' to call someone who will take my prayer requests to heart and will pray for me. I recall a time when my youngest child had a life-and-death health situation and my family and my church stood in the gap and prayed earnestly. Two weeks later there was a complete turnaround, a miracle of healing. Somebody touched God for me! Often we hear missionaries tell of dire situations, hopeless situations that resolved miraculously. Later they found out someone across the world was praying for them at that very moment.

Today each one reading this - Satan has desired you. He has attempted to sift you, but someone praying for you has made the difference. Your pastor wants you to make it.. and is praying for you. Your friends want you to make it…. and they are praying for you. The church is praying for you. But greater than all *...there is one God, and one mediator between God and men, the man Christ Jesus.* 1 Timothy 2:5 *He knows our frame… and he remembereth that we are dust.* Psalm 103:14 … *He is able also to save them to the uttermost that come unto God by him, seeing he ever liveth to make intercession...* Hebrews 7:25… *It is Christ that died, yea rather, that is risen again, who is even at the right hand of God, who also maketh intercession for us.* Romans 8:34 … *but the Spirit itself maketh intercession for us with groanings which cannot be uttered.* Romans 8:26.

Satan desired Simon Peter. Satan desires you. In this equation there are two constants, Jesus and Satan. There is only one variable - you. We have a formidable enemy from day one in the Garden of Eden. *And I will put enmity between thee and the woman, and between thy seed and her seed,* (Genesis 3:15).

We look today to Simon Peter as a prototype of our walk with God. Other than Jesus, no name comes up so often as Peter's name in the gospels. Jesus was tempted in all points, yet without sin. Peter was tempted in all points…and sometimes fell flat. Peter was intensely human.

There were violent and extreme contrasts in Peter's own nature: There were spiritual insights, prophetic utterances. Then there were words of denial and blasphemy. There were glaring failures but valiant triumphs. There was bravery and there was cowardice. We see the greatness of his strengths and the enormity of his mistakes. He received the severest rebuke of any of Christ's followers, yet he also received the highest words of approbation. He forsook all to follow Him - yet he forsakes Him in the garden.

Like the unbelievable contrasts in our own lives, he reminds us so much of our own failings: Our ups and downs, our "been there, done that…," our constantly making mistakes.

On a close study of his call, it appears there were at least two calls and perhaps three before Peter totally cast his lot to follow Jesus. Matthew tells of a call when Peter was fishing. Mark tells of a call to the four when they were mending their nets. Then there was a decisive time when Jesus taught from Peter's boat and then asked the fishermen to launch out into the deep and cast their nets. It was then that Peter forsook all and followed. Perhaps the first call was to believe, the second call to follow, the third call to forsake all. Even then we see a roller coaster/a see-saw in his actions and words.

There were great sacrifices: *Then Peter began to say unto him, Lo, we have left all, and have followed thee.* Mark 10:28

He had blinding, wonderful revelations, monumental experiences. *And Jesus answered and said unto him, Blessed art thou, Simon Barjona: for flesh and blood hath not revealed it unto thee, but my Father which is in heaven. And I say also unto thee, That thou art Peter, and upon this rock I will build my church; and the gates of hell shall not prevail against it. And I will give unto thee the keys of the kingdom of heaven:* Matthew 16:17-19

He made embarrassing goofs. Scholars think this incident was the very next day after receiving the keys. It was told in the same chapter. *From that time forth began Jesus to shew unto his disciples, how that he must go unto Jerusalem, and suffer many things of the elders and chief priests and scribes, and be killed, and be raised again the third day. Then Peter took him, and began to rebuke him, saying, Be it far from thee, Lord: this shall not be unto thee. But he turned, and said unto Peter, Get thee behind me, Satan: thou art an offence unto me: for thou savourest not the things that be of God, but those that be of men.* Matthew 16:21-23.

Concern for the coming rejection and sufferings of Jesus filled Peter with indignation and pain, and Peter in love said: *'Be it far from thee, Lord this shall not be unto thee.'* Jesus was not calling Peter Satan, but He directly confronted the enemy for his use of Peter in tempting Him to avoid the cross. Peter both blessed and cursed with his words - becoming the mouthpiece of His heavenly father on one occasion and a mouthpiece of Satan on another. He must have felt like a spiritual giant one moment and a grasshopper shortly after. It was sifting time.

Then the Mount of Transfiguration, what an experience

was his in the company of Moses, Elijah and Jesus! And Peter fell short again. *And Peter answered and said to Jesus, Master, it is good for us to be here: and let us make three tabernacles; one for thee, and one for Moses, and one for Elias. For he wist not what to say; for they were sore afraid.* Mark 9:5-6. Mark was a little kinder to his Uncle Peter *("he wist not what to say")* than Luke in recounting this incident. Luke said Peter *"... was not knowing what he said."* (Foot in mouth! Been there and done that!)

Peter had major errors in discernment, judgment, perception. Often we see his motives were right but his methods were wrong. *Then cometh he to Simon Peter: and Peter saith unto him, Lord, dost thou wash my feet? Jesus answered and said unto him, What I do thou knowest not now; but thou shalt know hereafter. Peter saith unto him, Thou shalt never wash my feet. Jesus answered him, If I wash thee not, thou hast no part with me. Simon Peter saith unto him, Lord, not my feet only, but also my hands and my head.* John 13:6-9 (You certainly cannot accuse Peter of being a hypocrite).

Jesus spoke words of approval and praise and even blessing to Simon Peter not spoken to any other, and in the same chapter harder things to Peter than He ever said to any other disciple.

Then came Peter to him, and said, Lord, how oft shall my brother sin against me, and I forgive him? till seven times? Matthew 18:21.

Oops, Satan will sift you over this, Peter. It would have been a poor outlook for Peter if Jesus had a numerical limit to forgiveness, no more than seven times. Had Jesus accepted Peter's limit of forgiveness, Peter would never have made it. Sinning and falling again and again, he needed the 70 x 7.

We see Peter's confidence in himself, then bumbling and

falling flat on his face. *Peter answered and said unto him, Though all men shall be offended because of thee, yet will I never be offended. Jesus said unto him, Verily I say unto thee, That this night, before the cock crow, thou shalt deny me thrice. Peter said unto him, Though I should die with thee, yet will I not deny thee. Likewise also said all the disciples.* Matthew 26:33-35 *But he spake the more vehemently, If I should die with thee, I will not deny thee in any wise.* Mark 14:27-31

Have you been there, done that? The very thing you said you wouldn't do: "That's my strong point! I would be the last one to do that." And you have to eat your own words! Satan will sift you with that one if he can. Peter was a brave man. When he said, Jesus I am ready to go with thee to prison and to death – he meant it.

Notice the passage in Luke: *And they said, Lord, behold, here are two swords. And he said unto them, It is enough.* Luke 22: 38 BUT *"... Then Simon Peter having a sword drew it, and smote the high priest's servant, and cut off his right ear. The servant's name was Malchus. Then said Jesus unto Peter, Put up thy sword into the sheath: the cup which my Father hath given me, shall I not drink it?* John 18:10-11

We see here a display of human devotion - a willingness to take risks. Peter draws his sword and impulsively leaps into the fray, ready to thrust at the enemy daring to injure his Lord. Now Peter experiences confusion and doubt: "But Jesus said we could take our two swords. I said 'I would die for Him.' I tried to defend Him, willing to fight for Him. I cut off the ear of one of the combatants – and He undid what I was trying to do. What do I do now?" He was shaken.

Time and time again, Peter had seen Jesus being delivered from His enemies' hands before. *And all they in the synagogue, when they heard these things, were filled with wrath, And rose up, and thrust him out of the city, and led him unto the brow of the hill whereon their city was built, that they might cast him down headlong. But he passing through the midst of them went his way,* Luke 4:28-30

Peter had been there and seen Him evade capture time and again, heal the sick, raise the dead, walk on water, calm storms. Jesus had told him to catch a fish for their taxes - and there was the miraculous supply of their need. He caught a miraculous abundance of fish at the word of the Lord after fishing all night and catching none. He had seen Him calm the seas, *What manner of man is this, that even the winds and sea obey?* Matthew 8:27. Now when it really came to the crunch, the most important time of all, was Jesus powerless? Peter's confidence was shaken. Was it that Jesus could not? Or was it that He would not? Now Peter was plunged into a need of trusting with the unexplained. Whether He could not or would not - it looks like He let Peter down! *"What I do thou knowest not now; but thou shalt know hereafter."*

Now we must think again of Peter's most notable failure – one that made the headlines - doing the one thing he said he would not do. *"Though all men shall be offended because of thee, yet will I never be offended." But he spake the more vehemently, "If I should die with thee, I will not deny thee in any wise."* This failure was broadcast in all four GOSPELS – how humiliating.

Satan's subtlety to destroy Peter's faith is seen in that he attempted the sifting of the apostle not with a soldier's threat but a little maid's off-hand derision. Not a big tough soldier – but a little maid - and Peter swore with many oaths that he did not even know Jesus. Peter forgot his discipleship, his vows, his Master – everything but his jeopardy.

Satan could have done a number on Simon Peter if he had let him. Every time Peter read Matthew's Gospel, Luke's

Gospel, Mark's Gospel, John's Gospel, every time he heard a rooster crow, it was a reminder.

So what was the most needful prayer for Peter?

Jesus could have told him, "I'm not praying that you be spared from humiliation or exposure of weakness. I'm not praying that you be without temptation or even failure. I am not praying that you be spared from confusion, from tests, from misunderstandings." (See Galatians 2:11). His prayer was not that Peter be spared misplaced confidence or imprisonment (one time Peter would be miraculously delivered and another time he would be left to suffer). He was not praying that Peter be spared from martyrdom. He prayed simply that his faith fail not. He knew Peter was going to fail sometimes and fail miserably... But He was still praying for him. "Peter, don't give up! I want you to make it. Satan desires to sift you. I have prayed for you."

All our failures, mistakes, failed expectations can nibble away at our faith. Gaping holes may appear where our faith was. "But I thought…."

We could go on and on. There were many more instances Peter's faith was attacked.

Someone Peter had confidence in failed *Then said Jesus unto him, That thou doest, do quickly. Now no man at the table knew for what intent he spake this unto him. For some of them thought, because Judas had the bag, that Jesus had said unto him, Buy those things that we have need of against the feast; or, that he should give something to the poor.* John 13:27-29.

And Peter, something is going to be required of you that is not required of everyone. (That has sifted many). *Verily, verily, I say unto thee, When thou wast young, thou girdest thyself, and walkedst whither thou wouldest: but when thou shalt be old, thou shalt stretch forth thy hands, and another shall gird thee, and carry thee whither thou wouldest not. This spake he, signifying by what death he should glorify God. And when he had spoken this, he saith unto him, Follow me. Then Peter, turning about, seeth the disciple whom Jesus loved following; which also leaned on his breast at supper, and said, Lord, which is he that betrayeth thee? Peter seeing him saith to Jesus, Lord, and what shall this man do? Jesus saith unto him, If I will that he tarry till I come, what is that to thee? follow thou me.* John 21:18-22

Peter had much to learn and unlearn – he was full of prejudices, misconceptions, i.e., the tangible versus the eternal, his methods (sword versus love), expecting here and now. *Wilt thou at this time restore again the kingdom to Israel?*

Consider: Elijah and John the Baptist were undoubtedly heroes of faith, but as we know, one's faith failed in the desert and the heart of the other failed him in prison. (John the Baptist: *Now when John had heard in the prison the works of Christ, he sent two of his disciples, And said unto him, Art thou he that should come, or do we look for another?* Matthew 11:2-3)
Consider Moses: *For he supposed his brethren would have understood how that God by his hand would deliver them: but they understood not.* Acts 7:25

We may have our pat answers: This is the way to get your healing. It happened this way for me before. This is the way to ensure victory. This is the way to keep your family together. It is much easier to have faith when we think we have the answers. Like the apostles, we can think erroneously "at this time."

Trouble may come. Trouble will come. Satan wants you and yours. Some days you will feel like you can walk on water and other days you will be sinking beyond all hope: "Lord, save me." Some days you will cry out "vehemently" “though all be offended, yet not I." Other days a subtle taunt in a social situation will bring forth an action (if not the words) of “I'm not one of them.” Some days it will be: "Let's build three tabernacles – and never go home." Other days: “Depart from me for I am a sinful man, O Lord.” But you do have what it takes. Someone is on your side. Someone is praying for you.

What Christ accomplished for Peter, he can do for us. How comforting! Not if - but when - you are converted, strengthen the brethren. When you have the victory, help someone else. "Thou art … thou shalt be…" Thou art – vacillating, impetuous Simon. Thou shalt be – Cephas a rock! And upon this rock….. I WILL!

My help cometh from the LORD, which made heaven and earth. He will not suffer thy foot to be moved: he that keepeth thee will not slumber. Psalm 121:2-3

Jesus knew the weak and strong points of Peter and He knows mine, but He will not let go. It is a foregone conclusion of victory if I hang in there. It is up to me. I will either be a trophy of Satan or a monument to the grace of God.

And I give unto them eternal life; and they shall never perish, neither shall any man pluck them out of my hand. My Father, which gave them me, is greater than all; and no man is able to pluck them out of my Father's hand. John 10:28-29

You are safe if you don't give up, if your faith fail not… despite all your faults of temperament, all defects of character, all the scandals of conduct. The bad news is Satan desires you. The good news is, Someone is praying for you. "*I pray not that thou shouldest take them out of the world, but that thou shouldest keep them from the evil. Neither pray I for these alone, but for them also which shall believe on me through their word.* John 17: 15, 20

Satan is trying to crush you. You may get bruised but he is the one that will be crushed. (Genesis 3:15)

Behold, I give unto you power to tread on serpents and scorpions, and over all the power of the enemy: and nothing shall by any means hurt you. Luke 10:19

When you have it made.... strengthen the brethren. . .

For I am persuaded, that neither death, nor life, nor angels, nor principalities, nor powers, nor things present, nor things to come, Nor height, nor depth, nor any other creature, shall be able to separate us from the love of God, which is in Christ Jesus our Lord. Romans 8:38, 39

Wherefore he is able also to save them to the uttermost that come unto God by him, seeing he ever liveth to make intercession for them. Hebrews 7:25

Someone is praying for you that your faith fail not!

Peter looking back wrote: *That the trial of your faith, being much more precious than of gold that perisheth, though it be tried with fire, might be found unto praise and honour and glory at the appearing of Jesus Christ: Whom having not seen, ye love; in whom, though now ye see him not, yet believing, ye rejoice with joy unspeakable and full of glory: Receiving the <u>end</u> of your faith, even the salvation of your <u>souls</u>.* 1 Peter 1:7-9

Others May, You Cannot

If God has called you to be really like Jesus, He will draw you into a life of crucifixion and humility, and put upon you such demands of obedience that you will not be able to follow other people, or measure yourself by other Christians, and in many ways He will seem to let other good people do things which He will not let you do.

Other Christians and ministers, who seem to be very religious and useful, may push themselves, pull wires, and work schemes to carry out their plans, but you cannot do it, and if you do, you will meet with such failure and rebuke from the Lord as will make you sorely penitent.

Others may boast of themselves, of their work, of their success, of their writings, but the Holy Spirit will not allow you to do any such things; and if you begin it, He will lead you into some deep mortification that will make you despise yourself and all your good works.

Others may be allowed to succeed in making money, or have a legacy left to them; but it is likely God will keep you poor, because He wants you to have something far better than gold, namely, a helpless dependence on Him, that He may have the privilege of supplying your need out of an unseen treasury.

The Lord may let others be honored and put forward, and keep you hidden in obscurity, because He wants to produce some choice, fragrant fruit for His coming glory, which can only be produced in the shade. He may let others be great but keep you small.

He may let others do a work for Him and get the credit for it, but He will make you work and toil without knowing how much you are doing; and then to make your work still more precious, HE may let others get the credit for work which you have done, and thus make your reward ten times greater when Jesus comes.

The Holy Spirit will put a strict watch over you, with a jealous love, and will rebuke you for little words and feelings, or for wasting your time and money, which other Christians never seem distressed over.

So, make up your mind that God is an infinite Sovereign, and has a right to do as He pleases with His own. He may not explain to you a thousand things which may puzzle your reason in His dealings with you; but if you absolutely sell yourself to be His love slave, He will wrap you in a jealous love, and bestow upon you many blessings which come only to those who are in the inner circle.

Settle it forever, then, that you are to deal directly with the Holy Spirit, and that He is to have the privilege of tying your tongue, or chaining your hand, or closing your eyes, in ways that He does not seem to use with others. Now, when you are so possessed with the living God that you are, in your secret heart, pleased and delighted over this peculiar, personal, private, jealous guardianship, and management of the Holy Spirit over your life, you will have found the vestibule to Heaven.

Author Unknown

References:

Much of this synopsis of the Life of Peter was inspired by and gleaned from All the Apostles of the Bible, written by Herbert Lockyer, and published by Zondervan Publishing House, Grand Rapids, Michigan 1972

Recommended Resources:

That Your Faith Fail Not PowerPoint is available on request to mwolfe242@aol. com, no charge.

LIFE APPLICATION

1. Do you think Jesus' commendation of Peter in Matthew 16:17-19 emboldened him to speak up in verse 22 and contradict Jesus 'Nay, Lord... Not so.'

2. Has there been a time in your life of when high moment of approbation for spiritual sensitivity was followed immediately by a crass failure of yours and being humiliated by rebuke? Were you more vulnerable after great revelation and great resolve? Was this a trial of faith for you?

3. Do you think Jesus' comment about swords could have been a factor in Peter using his sword in the garden? Could Peter have taken offense over the rebuke "Put up thy sword... "

4. From a human standpoint list the occasions in Peter's life that you can see that Peter was called upon to "trust God with the unexplained."

5. Think of the rebukes Peter received in the Bible.

Directed to all the apostles? Ye of little faith...., Ye know not what spirit ye are of?, etc.

Peter singled out individually?

6. What can we learn from Peter's "come back" after his faith failed him? Why do you think Jesus told the women after the resurrection, "tell my apostles and Peter...."? Do you think Peter needed this personal affirmation after his flagrant public failure and denial?

7. Find scriptures in Peter's epistles (1 and 2 Peter) that show Peter's faith was triumphant in the end and that his faith did not fail.

NOTES:

IT'S JUST NOT FAIR

My niece was choosing a Bible story to read her toddler, and she chose "Daniel in the Lion's Den." He objected and in a quivering voice said, "There's a little part of my heart that doesn't like that story."

I must admit, I have some favorite passages in the Bible and there are some that are NOT my favorites. Some parables I do not fully understand and there are some verses hard to accept. There is even a popular book on "The Hard Sayings of the Bible." There are times when people ask me for my interpretation of certain passages, and often I must say, "I just don't know."

Jesus many times called aside the disciples and explained deeper meanings of the parables. After one parable Jesus even said, "Know ye not this parable? and how then will ye know all parables?" (i.e., You must get this one.) Sometimes it is with age, experiences, trials, and yes, chastisement, we learn meanings. As one parent said when disciplining his child, "Sometimes you just have to explain it more better." Life has a way of "explaining it better."

Don't get it wrong: The way of salvation is certainly not obscure to those who seek.

> *"Wherever the Word touches upon vital points, it is as bright as a sunbeam. Mysteries there are, and profound doctrines; but where it has to do with that which concerns us for eternity, it is so plain that the babe in grace may safely wade in its refreshing streams. The wayfaring man, though a fool, need not err from the right path."* (*Called, Chosen & Faithful*, Search for Truth Publications, Houston, TX)

Mark Twain is supposed to have said: *"It ain't the parts of the Bible that I can't understand that bother me, it is the parts that I do understand."*

Matthew 20:1-14 relates a parable told by Jesus. I do not remember ever hearing an expository sermon on this particular parable, just brief mentions, and simply reading it has often left me perplexed. In fact, frankly for a long time "there was a little part of my heart that did not like this story."

1 For the kingdom of heaven is like unto a man that is an householder, which went out early in the morning to hire labourers into his vineyard.

2 And when he had agreed with the labourers for a penny a day, he sent them into his vineyard. (Penny: a denarius, principal silver coin of the Roman empire. It appears it was then the ordinary pay for a day's wages.)

3 And he went out about the third hour, (9 a.m.) *and saw others standing idle in the marketplace,*

4 And said unto them; Go ye also into the vineyard, and whatsoever is right I will give you. And they went their way.

5 Again he went out about the sixth and ninth hour, (12 and 3 p.m.) *and did likewise.*

6 And about the eleventh hour (5 p.m.) *he went out, and found others standing idle, and saith unto them, Why stand ye here all the day idle?*

7 They say unto him, Because no man hath hired us. He saith unto them, Go ye also into the vineyard; and whatsoever is right, that shall ye receive.

8 So when even was come, the lord of the vineyard saith unto his steward, Call the labourers, and give them their hire, beginning from the last unto the first.

9 And when they came that were hired about the eleventh hour, they received every man a penny.
10 But when the first came, they supposed that they should have received more; and they likewise received every man a penny.
11 And when they had received it, they murmured against the goodman of the house,
12. Saying, These last have wrought but one hour, and thou hast made them equal unto us, which have borne the burden and heat of the day. (Do the grumblers have our sympathy? Do they not have a bona fide complaint?)
13 But he answered one of them, and said, Friend, I do thee no wrong: didst not thou agree with me for a penny?
14 Take that thine is, and go thy way: I will give unto this last, even as unto thee.
15 Is it not lawful for me to do what I will with mine own? Is thine eye evil, because I am good?
16 So the last shall be first, and the first last: for many be called, but few chosen.

CONSIDER

- *He is only an owner in name who has no right to do as he will with his own. Amy Carmichael*
- *Is it not lawful for me to do what I will with mine own?* Matthew 20:1-14.
- *For my thoughts are not your thoughts, neither are your ways my ways, saith the* LORD. *For as the heavens are higher than the earth, so are my ways higher than your ways, and my thoughts than your thoughts.* Isaiah 55:8-9

Despite these favorite quotes of mine, a little part of me doesn't like this story. I am not alone. Many theologians say this is perhaps the hardest parable to interpret. There are many different takes. Obviously, Jesus was not telling us to run our businesses like this. Some scholars say perhaps the 11th-hour laborers did as much in one hour as the others did in 12, but in that event the householder probably would have told them, "they got as much done as you did." Others try to reason: maybe the first ones got a brass penny, the second ones a silver and the last ones a gold one – but then there would have been no complaint in verse 12: "*Saying, These last have wrought but one hour, and thou hast made them equal unto us, which have borne the burden and heat of the day.*"

The central concern from this parable is one of fairness: "That's just not fair." We like equality and parity and when life is otherwise, we are disturbed and cry, "Not fair! I don't understand!" It's not that we mind them getting blessed. We do not mind God being generous and giving them the penny, but not equal to what we got. We did get what was promised to us, but shouldn't we get more if we did more? We readily understand the scriptural principles, "You reap what you sow," "If you don't work, you don't eat," etc. That's fair! But "Thou hast made them equal unto us" just doesn't fit our sense of justice.

Psychologists say the root of anger is most often a feeling of unfairness coupled with a feeling of helplessness or the inability to do anything about it. Our earliest social sense has to do with fairness. As kids, we cried, "Why does she get one and I didn't? That's not fair," or "her piece is larger than mine." As a mother, we find it quite challenging to make sure we are fair: equal gifts, same rules, same rewards, equal treatment. One father, instead of trying to make sure everything was fair and equal, told his child, "You're never gonna get the same things as other people. It's never going to be equal. It is not going to happen ever in your life so you must learn that now. Listen, the only time you should look in your neighbor's bowl is to make sure they have enough. You don't look in your neighbor's bowl to see if you have as much as them."

Many families quarrel when dividing up inheritance: "I took care of mom and dad," or "mom and dad helped you more, they gave you more money," "it's not fair." And like the young man in Luke 12:13, we expect Jesus to intervene and get us our fair shake: *Master, speak to my brother, that he divide the inheritance with me.*

We are supposed to get what we deserve, isn't that right, surely? We hear so often today, "everybody deserves such-and-such (education, a house, access to care, a good job, minimum wage, happiness, marriage, etc.)

Consider these humorous stories about getting what one deserves:

- One man who responded to being honored in a public forum. "I don't appreciate this, but I sure do deserve it." (A Freudian slip?)
- Another lady said about deserving her award: "I don't deserve this. But I have arthritis: I don't deserve that either."
- When an artist revealed his commissioned portrait to one lady, she exclaimed: "This doesn't do me justice." The artist replied, "Lady, you don't need justice, you need mercy."

We will tell our children, our friends, "Well, life just isn't fair," with a lecturing tone, but down deep we are thinking, "yes, but it should be." We wish we could understand. Someone gets sick, someone young dies, someone has a horrible accident, it's just "not fair." Like perfect Job, our desire is that the Almighty would answer us and explain.

When my life was touched in a short span of time by the death of a grandchild, unbelievable suffering of another grandchild, a disabling accident of my husband, criminal robbery and assault on a close member of my family, a dear friend said, "It's not fair, Mary doesn't deserve this." This was a salve to my hurt and comforted me somewhat. It is easy to feel a sense of abandonment and betrayal when we receive unexplained troubles, when we feel we played by the rules and got penalized. Like Job, we want an umpire - Job 9:33: *"Neither is there any daysman betwixt us, that might lay his hand upon us both."* Frustration, confusion, disillusionment can set in with dangerous consequences to our spiritual health - and pain and suffering are not the greatest damage. Loss of confidence is.

How do we explain apparent injustices, the disparities of life? Some people experience lifelong hardships and injustice; others seem to enjoy every blessing. We just don't get it. Like one discouraged soul, we feel, "I've seen something King David didn't see. I've seen the righteous forsaken. It's not fair."

Look at our parable closely today. The all-day workers had it tough. They looked around and saw only unfairness. They had worked 12 hours and got the same pay as the one-hour workers. On the surface, we would say they had a valid grievance to take to the union.

Most of you reading this book have been faithful many, many years. Many of you know the feeling of toiling tirelessly while others lag behind. On the surface, it appears to you that others got a free pass. You perhaps feel you have worked hard for what came easy for someone else.

In another parable, most of us can identify with the prodigal son's elder brother. He stayed and worked on the family farm, but no one threw him a party. In fact, no one even let him know about the party for his brother. Life surely had been more difficult for him because his brother had run away from responsibility. He had to do the work of two. To him, it probably appeared his brother's life had been a party while he was working his youth away.

Back to the saga in Matthew 20. There are many lessons we can learn.

These all-day workers got exactly what they bargained for, (the going rate), and exactly what they were expecting, (they "agreed with the labourers for a penny a day,) but they were still unhappy. They were angry that others got a better deal. We identify with them. Sometimes others get recompense, recognition or honor that appear undeserved. We want the same breaks, especially if we have worked harder and served more faithfully.

When we have this attitude, we have a lot of company, even the wise Solomon said it like this: *Then said I in my heart, As it happeneth to the fool, so it happeneth even to me; and why was I then more wise? Then I said in my heart, that this also is vanity. Ecclesiastes 2:15*

I have driven by large estates that I knew their gain was ill-gotten. They had cheated and bilked the federal government, but they were honored and esteemed in the community because of their wealth. My heart said, "Not fair. Just one of their fancy cars cost more than I make with a year of hard, honest labor." Unfairness irks us. Bosses get honors and big bonuses because of work we did for them. We just don't want someone else to get something we think we deserve.

But, let's reconsider: Although I feel a kinship to the exasperated all-day workers, when I look closely the group I should most relate to is the last group, those who were offered a full pay even though they hadn't worked a full load.

Let's think a little bit about the heat of the day and who has worked the hardest. Do I really want fairness? Do I want payment to be divvied out accordingly to what effort and sacrifice were expended? Do I want to be graded on the curve?

What about the generation before mine? My dad walked miles to school and church. Their church services were often in brush arbors or tents, in scorching heat or bitter cold, with mosquitoes, maybe even snakes. They were ridiculed, bombarded with rotten tomatoes and sometimes more dangerous projectiles. Their lives were sometimes threatened. Gospel groups traveled to bring the truth to areas with no preacher. They often had to sleep on the ground, floor or hard benches. I know of more than one evangelistic party that told of times they would go hungry. One group told of subsisting for days on just cornflakes to eat.

Many of them were ridiculed and ostracized. Many of them had to choose between family members and the gospel. It's not fair. I signed on in the 11th hour. The gospel has been preached for decades in my community. I did not have to forsake family. I was never really persecuted, maybe mocked a little, reproached, but I am accepted. I did not have to go against family, public opinion. I know some that have but not me. I have always known the plan of salvation, the name of Jesus. I've always had access to the Bible. So do I get the same pay as those who did not? Do I want fairness?

The story of my life is more like the following passage.

And it shall be, when the Lord thy God shall give thee great and goodly cities, which thou buildedst not, And houses full of all good things, which thou filledst not, and wells digged, which thou diggedst not, vineyards and olive trees, which thou plantedst not; when thou shalt have eaten and be full; Then beware lest thou forget the Lord, which brought thee forth out of the land of Egypt, from the house of bondage. Deuteronomy 6:10-12

What of the hordes of workers even today in his vineyard that do not live in the United States. Some live in the midst of wars; their country has not known peace for generations. Talk about working in the heat of the day! Some live in famine; it is said 1 billion people, or 1 in 6, will go to bed hungry tonight, and I have never had to go hungry. Some are the only Christians in their community, in their family. Many do not have a Bible. Almost 2,000 language groups do not have a single verse of Scripture available in their languages.

Let's talk more about fairness. It's not fair that I live where there is freedom. Yes, I know that is fragile right now, but I still have freedom. You mean I am going to get eternal life with those that worship in dire jeopardy, with those that play volley ball with half of the congregation to cover the noise while the others have church service and worship.

Do I get paid eternal life alongside the martyred Christians in our generation - tortured, even beheaded for their beliefs? Do I get a crown of faithfulness alongside the missionaries that have left all to go to a foreign land? Is that fair? Am I to be treated equally?

The disciples were needy in every way. They had no security, no property to call their own. They also had no New Testament as an instruction manual. To answer His call, they gave up everything which could have given them security in this life. Tradition tells us all were persecuted, that 11 of the 12 died martyr deaths. What about it, Mary? Made equal with them? You, an 11th-hour end-of-the-day worker? Are you going to receive eternal life alongside them? As Brother Paul said, "Ye have not yet resisted unto blood, striving against sin." Hebrews 12:4

This was not the first time God was accused that his ways were not just. We find the same kind of thinking in Ezekiel 18:26-29:

> *When a righteous man turneth away from his righteousness, and committeth iniquity, and dieth in them; for his iniquity that he hath done shall he die. Again, when the wicked man turneth away from his wickedness that he hath committed, and doeth that which is lawful and right, he shall save his soul alive. Because he considereth, and turneth away from all his transgressions that he hath committed, he shall surely live, he shall not die. Yet saith the house of Israel, The way of the Lord is not equal. O house of Israel, are not my ways equal? are not your ways unequal?*

Yes, God loves justice and fairness, in fact, *"Justice and judgment are the habitation of His throne..."* Psalm 89:14 but there is another factor in His economy: God's grace and mercy.

> *"There is nothing little in God; his mercy is like himself--it is infinite. You cannot measure it. His mercy is so great that it forgives great sins to great sinners, after great lengths of time, and then gives great favours and great privileges, and raises us up to great enjoyments in the great heaven of the great God. It is undeserved mercy,*

as indeed all true mercy must be, for deserved mercy is only a misnomer for justice." (Spurgeon)

But thou, O Lord, art a God full of compassion, and gracious, long suffering, and plenteous in mercy and truth. Psalm 86:15

On reflection, I am oh so glad today that God doesn't just give us what we deserve. Yes, I had troubles I didn't deserve, but even more so, I have had countless blessings I didn't earn. When I grieve and have regrets because I did not come up to what was expected in some area in my life, I can rejoice. Today is the first day of the rest of my life. The last mile is what counts. "As a tree falls so shall it lie." I can still work on it.

> *Seek ye the Lord while he may be found, call ye upon him while he is near: Let the wicked forsake his way, and the unrighteous man his thoughts: and let him return unto the Lord, and he will have mercy upon him; and to our God, for he will abundantly pardon. For my thoughts are not your thoughts, neither are your ways my ways, saith the Lord. For as the heavens are higher than the earth, so are my ways higher than your ways, and my thoughts than your thoughts.*
> Isaiah 55:6-9

Have you desired to work in His vineyard? He is still looking, "Who will work for me today?" Today is the first day of the rest of your life. You can still get in on His great mercies.

Yes, <u>life is not fair</u>: Rejoice, sinner friend:
While we were yet sinners! Christ died for us.
<u>Life is not fair</u>: Praise the Lord, you that have failed:

His mercies are new every morning!
Life is not fair: Rejoice all you with loved ones and children unsaved.

His mercy endures forever! *And there is hope in thine end, saith the Lord, that thy children shall come again to their own border.* Jeremiah 31:16

> *He will turn again, he will have compassion upon us; he will subdue our iniquities; and thou wilt cast all their sins into the depths of the sea.* Micah 7:19

> *"For my thoughts are not your thoughts, neither are your ways my ways, saith the Lord. For as the heavens are higher than the earth, so are my ways higher than your ways, and my thoughts than your thoughts."* Isaiah 55:8-9

An old man expressed a desire to repent, but remarked it wasn't fair to turn to God in his later years, that he had wasted his life. He was told, "That's what grace is all about."

Now, instead of "there's a little part of my heart that doesn't like that story," I love this parable! It is the 11th hour, but there is still time for everyone to come on board. You may have to work for just one hour, but He is calling, "Who will go and work for me today? Why do you sit idle?" He will give unto these late comers the gift of eternal life. I say in my heart today, "Life is not fair - and I am oh, so glad! Life is not fair - praise the Lord."

Understand this: His mercy and grace and blessings to someone else does not take one thing from me. There is plenty to go around.

Perhaps there is another principle here. The ones that came first were working for what they could get. "*And when he had agreed with the labourers for a penny a day, he sent them into his vineyard."* All the others were trusting and went willingly to work with His promise of "whatsoever is right, that shall ye receive." Contrast their spirits. Let us take care that we do not work with a mere hireling spirit, a "what's in it for me" attitude? Our prayers, our service, our church attendance will be small in the eyes of God if we are just doing it for pay. We already have our reward if we do it for the recompense or recognition we get out of it. The hagglers, the bargainers got what they agreed for. The trusting laborers got far more than they were expecting. Rather than worrying about getting our dues, focusing on personal justice and fairness, we must do our part to get the work done before the sun sets. Trust His generosity. " Shall not the Judge of all the earth do right?" (Genesis 18:25)

> *Go ye also into the vineyard, and whatsoever is right I will give you.*
> *Go ye also into the vineyard; and whatsoever is right, that shall ye receive.*

Trust him! Claim every promise, but don't keep a tally God is a good accountant. He numbers the hairs of our head; even our tears are bottled up.

To the most of you who have worked through the heat of the day. Don't quit now. Thou shalt be recompensed! Dear elder brother: you have a place at the table, at the party. Everything He has is thine. The same love He showed to the prodigal son, the Father portrays to you. "...therefore came his father out, and intreated him... And he said unto him, Son, thou art ever with me, and all that I have is thine." Party hearty!

For God is not unrighteous to forget your work and labour of love, which ye have shewed toward his name, in that ye have ministered to the saints, and do minister. And we desire that every one of you do shew the same diligence to the full assurance of hope unto the end: That ye be not slothful, but followers of them who through faith and patience inherit the promises. Hebrews 6:10-12

For ye have need of patience, that, after ye have done the will of God, ye might receive the promise. Hebrews 10:36

And let the peace of God rule in your hearts, to the which also ye are called in one body; and be ye thankful. Colossians 3:15

I love the attitude of one precious saint: "It was told that as he worshipped his Lord, the Saviour appeared and said, "You have served me well, what reward shall I give thee for thy work?" Whereupon he answered, “Nothing but thyself, O Lord.” God Himself is our exceeding great reward.

LIFE APPLICATION

1. Consider the parable of the talents. What do we learn from the same reward the servants received even though their outcomes were not the same. "Faithful over a few things, Ruler over many."

2. List the most precious things you have received, perhaps the love of a companion, stability of a family, a nice home, financial security, a storybook childhood. Were you more deserving than some you know that have not had those particular blessings?

3. Do you agree with the philosophy of the father who told his child, "The only time you should look in your neighbor's bowl is to make sure they have enough? You don't look in your neighbor's bowl to see if you have as much as them."

4. Think about Stephen and James cut off at the very beginning of their activity. Will they be rewarded side-by-side with Paul who toiled and experienced 40 years of suffering for Christ? With John who is thought to have lived to an age of more than 100 years and suffered persecutions through much of them?

5. Write out the scriptures that we can count on that there is full recompense, that what is "right" He will give us. (Luke 4:14, Matthew 10:41,42; Hebrews 6:10, Galatians 6:9, Psalm7:13-14.)

6. Read Psalm 73. The psalmist was dealing with this feeling of unfairness. How was it resolved? Psalm 73:17-24.

<u>Resources and Recommendations:</u>

Note: A blog I read years ago on the internet helped so much my perspective on this parable. How I wish I had made note of the blog in its entirety and the author's name to give her recognition here. Many thoughts here were expanded from that blog - and "it's not fair" that I get all the credit. I would love to acknowledge her contribution.

It's Just Not Fair PowerPoint available on request to mwolfe242@aol.com (no charge)

WHERE CAN I GO?

And I said, Oh that I had wings like a dove! for then would I fly away, and be at rest. Lo, then would I wander far off, and remain in the wilderness. Selah. I would hasten my escape from the windy storm and tempest. Psalm 55:6-8

Can you relate to the psalmist here? Have you ever felt like running into the woods? Have there been times you had a temporary inclination just to keep driving? Have you ever said, "I'd like to take a slow boat to China." Or maybe you just wish you could hide in a dark box in a dark closet. If so, this lesson is for you.

With the psalmist, you cry in your heart: "*...Oh, that I had wings like a dove! I would fly away and be at rest. Indeed, I would wander far off, And remain in the wilderness. Selah. (NKJV)* Maybe you had just fleeting thoughts or perhaps you seriously contemplated throwing in the towel, skipping town, running away. Most of us would admit there are - or have been - times we would like to "split," call it quits, cop out, get away from it all – temporarily or forever. All of us are vulnerable and stressed out at times and life just becomes too much. You can relate to someone's tweet: If you can stay calm, while all around you is chaos, then you probably haven't completely understood the situation.

Perhaps there is someone specifically today that feels unappreciated and at the back of your mind is the thought, "I've had it. I don't have to take this." You feel like the hitchhiker that had a sign that stated, "Anywhere but here."

My husband's grandmother had a favorite saying for those who lives had become overwhelming, their housework just more than they could do, their home past redemption in her eyes: "I'd set fire to it and run away by the light of it."

Another of our family connections when times got tough would supposedly go for a loaf of bread and would stay away for a couple of weeks. I confess, once I bought a book "Where Does a Mother Go to Resign?" Not that I seriously thought about it, but it would be nice to know if I could abdicate. Where could I go and get away from it all?

When I was a child, there was a popular country song sung by Hank Williams: "Stop the world and let me off. I'm tired of going round and round." The psalmist expressed all these sentiments well when he penned: And I said, Oh that I had wings like a dove! for then would I fly away, and be at rest.

Most of you could probably tell of funny episodes when as a child you decided to escape and the realization you confronted when asked, "Where are you going to go?" Others know of tragic stories of runaway teenagers or young adults. There have been incidents of some even faking their death and starting a new life elsewhere. There are runaways in mid-life crises; there are elderly runaways. No age is immune. There is no typical runaway, no one precipitating factor. The danger was not so much in the act of running away, but where they ran to.

> There is a national switchboard for runaways and their statistics for one year were as follows: Causes for running away: Family Dynamics 42.4%, Peers/Social 14.2%, Youth Services 7.6%, School/Education 7.2%, Mental Health 6.4%, Alcohol/Drug Use 4.6%, Physical Abuse 3.8%, Judicial System 3.0%, Emotional/Verbal/Abuse 2.4%, Transportation 2.2%

I remember reading one of the most confounding missing person cases in a book by Max Lucado (*On the Anvil*, publisher Tyndale House Publishers, Inc,) A 45--year-old

Joseph Carter waved good-bye to friends after an evening meal in a NY restaurant, flagged down a taxi and rode off. He was never seen or heard from again. Many years of research offered countless theories but no conclusions. Since he was a successful NY Supreme Court Judge, many options have been presented – murder, kidnapping, Mafia involvement, even suicide. A search of his apartment revealed one clue. It was a note to his wife attached to a sizeable check. The note simply read: "I am very weary, Love Joe." For some of you, you are the journey has been long, the burdens are heavy, illusions have been shattered. You are weary. You are tired. You could say with Judge Carter: I am very weary.

You could say with the psalmist: Oh that I had wings like a dove. Some of you – it's not severe money problems, relentless pain, or harsh treatment. Life is just too daily. It's the tediousness of it all that has gotten to you. "If I could just wander off and remain in the wilderness. . . "

Very nearly since the time of creation we see this. Cain could not face his actions and decided to be a vagabond. It is certainly not appalling that you want to run and hide, but where you go and hide is critical.

Psychologists consider that one's judgment is intact if one realizes the likely outcome of one's actions. None of us will live long enough to learn every lesson from experience nor would we want to learn every lesson from experience. It has been well said, "Good judgment comes from bad experience and a lot of that comes from bad judgment."

To have good judgment, to know the likely outcome of our actions, we learn from observation, from experience, from history, and from the Bible. There is a parallel in the Book for every situation we face or a principle we can apply.

For whatsoever things were written aforetime were written for our learning, that we through patience and comfort of the scriptures might have hope. Romans 15:4

By study and application, we can ascertain the likely outcome of our actions. The most famous runaway in the Bible is probably the prodigal son, the boy that ran away from home. Why did he run away? The scriptures do not tell us and I have never heard a sermon speculating about this. Perhaps it was a disagreement with his brother, a strained relationship with his father, maybe rejection by a girlfriend, or all of the above. The why is not the heart of the matter. Most likely he grew tired of duty, day in and day out, the work on the farm. Possibly he was tired of responsibility or tired of the mundane. One day concluded, "There's got to be more." The grass looked greener on the other side… "I'm out of here!!!" Sounds pretty good, prodigal, but where are you going to go? Whither shall you flee?

"The younger son gathered all together, and took his journey into a far country…" Luke 15:13. The path from the Father's house always, always leads to a "far country" and then inevitably to the pig pen.

Let's fast forward a few weeks, months, maybe years. When the pigpen became too much, once again. I'm out of here *"I will arise and go…"* Luke 15:18. Where to now? Where are you going to go? *"I will arise and go to my father."* And he speculated on the likely outcome of that decision: *"…and (I) will say unto him, Father, I have sinned against heaven, and before thee, And am no more worthy to be called thy son: make me as one of thy hired servants.* V. 18 and 19.

There is an Old Testament parallel - a wayward daughter.

We do know her reason. While the prodigal son probably ran away from duty, she ran away from want, from a situation. Naomi *"went to sojourn in the country of Moab,"* a far country… because *"there was a famine in the land."* Ruth 1:1. She and her husband with their two sons ran away to Moab, to sojourn (to live temporarily). They took a trip. They ran away in a time of discouragement, a time of want.

When there is any famine in our lives, a time of trouble, or want, Satan always says, "run," if not physically, run away emotionally, mentally, spiritually. "Leave the Father's House. Flee as a bird to your mountain."

> *In the LORD put I my trust: how say ye to my soul, Flee as a bird to your mountain? For, lo, the wicked bend their bow, they make ready their arrow upon the string, that they may privily shoot at the upright in heart.* Psalm 11:1-2

Satan wants us to flee, to leave the protection of the House of God, the people of God so that he may privily shoot at the upright in heart. He wants us to leave the safety net of our Father's house and our comrades.

The meaning of Bethlehem was "house of bread." How ironic, Naomi left the "house of bread" in search of bread. In her anxiety about the future where it looked like no end to this tunnel, Naomi took a dead-end street. We see indicators that Naomi was a worrier: She named one son Mahlon, meaning the invalid or the sickly one, the other son Chilion, meaning wasting away/pining away. Then again they may have been sickly. She may have been obsessive and knew they had special needs. She desired security in the time of famine.

"Worry forms a channel into which everything else is drained."

For all of us, there will be times of famine. There will be times of want for different things in our lives. Peter says succinctly: "...*knowing that the same afflictions are accomplished in your brethren that are in the world.* 1 Peter 5:9

More important than the fact that there is a famine is our reaction, our response, how we determine to “fix it.” The fact that we need a refuge is not as weighty as where we decide to go, what will be the likely outcome to our actions. It is so easy to forget what we have and concentrate on what we are missing. Our wants become paramount.

If we listen to Satan, he always focuses us on what we do not have, what we cannot have. ... *Yea, hath God said, Ye shall not eat of every tree of the garden?* Genesis 3:1. He rephrased what God said putting the focus on what they could not have. What God had said was, *Of every tree of the garden thou mayest freely eat: But of the tree of the knowledge of good and evil, thou shalt not eat of it:* Genesis 2:16-17

Of every tree, Adam and Eve you may eat: The oranges, peaches, plums, kumquats, olives, dates, kiwi, pomegranate, pecan, grapefruit, almonds, nectarines, and on and on, *thou mayest freely eat.* Satan spotlighted the one thing they couldn't have.

Whatever we do not have (emotional needs, social needs, spiritual needs, physical needs), he tempts us, "if you will just disobey... leave your church, leave your family, leave your commitment, leave your consecrations, dedication, and convictions, you can have it." He always focuses on the area of famine, wanting us to forget what we have.

> *“The most unhappy of all men is he who believes himself to be so.”*

With all the fabulous possessions Solomon had, he said, “I hated life.... “ Ecclesiastes 2:17

Sometimes our famine is social, loneliness. *I looked on my right hand, and beheld, but there was no man that would know me: refuge failed me; no man cared for my soul.* Psalm 142:4

Sometimes physical, financial: *In weariness and painfulness, in watchings often, in hunger and thirst, in fastings often, in cold and nakedness.* 2 Corinthians 11:27

Sometimes it is a spiritual famine, a dry place in our walk with God. Job said: *Behold, I go forward, but he is not there; and backward, but I cannot perceive him: On the left hand, where he doth work, but I cannot behold him: he hideth himself on the right hand, that I cannot see him:* Job 23:8-9 Isaiah said: *And I will wait upon the Lord, that hideth his face from the house of Jacob, and I will look for him.* Isaiah 8: 17

In all these times, Satan says: "Flee to the mountains…." He tempts us to run away from the House of Bread in search of bread.

Naomi went to sojourn, (definition "a temporary stay"), but *they came into the country of Moab, and continued there.* Ruth 1:2. Possibly things went better for a while. Little Mahlon and Chilion (the invalid and the sickly) perhaps ate better than their cousins in Israel. But the result was the likely one: Naomi lost the very things she was trying to save in leaving the house of bread.

O Lord, I know that the way of man is not in himself: it is not in man that walketh to direct his steps. Jeremiah 10:23

There is a way which seemeth right unto a man, but the end thereof are the ways of death. Proverbs 14:12

And Elimelech Naomi's husband died; and she was left… Ruth 1:3 *And Mahlon and Chilion died also both of them; and the woman was left of her two sons and her husband.* Ruth 1:5

Now she is tormented with "If only…." and "What if." If only: Regrets over the past. What if: Worry over the future. But one day – like the prodigal – she came to herself. "I was arise and go to my Father's house."

Then she arose with her daughters in law, that she might return from the country of Moab: for she had heard in the country of Moab how that the LORD had visited his people in giving them bread. Ruth 1:6

Notice what Naomi says: *I went out full and the Lord hath brought me home again empty.* Ruth 1:21. She thought at that time she was empty, she was hungry. She forgot all she had. She ran after what she did not have and lost what she had. I've seen it so many times.

She returned with scars – she lost what she had "sojourned for" but there was restoration. This time she carefully considered "Where can I go?" *"Wherefore she went forth out of the place where she was and … went on the way to return unto the land of Judah.* Ruth 1:7

There is a danger in running without considering your destination. *As if a man did flee from a lion, and a bear met him; or went into the house, and leaned his hand on the wall, and a serpent bit him.* Amos 5:19 One needs to make sure the destination is a haven, a refuge. One needs to reflect on what happened to others who went this way, what happened over the long haul.

I was reminded of a little dog we had when our children were small. They called him a wiener dog, but this was a misnomer. He looked more like a corn dog, roly-poly, with short, short legs, very lazy and slow. But there was one thing that would make him move quickly. For some reason he was terrified of storms. He would be safe in his usual, cozy spot on the porch, but if a storm approached, he grew more and more restless and then would begin cowering and quivering. Finally his fear would become too much for him, perhaps intensified by a particularly virulent clap of thunder or a falling tree limb, and it would propel him from his shelter. He would run as fast as his short little legs could carry him pell-mell into the storm as though he could outrun it all. And all of the time, he could have remained dry, warm and safe.

> *Hear, O heavens, and give ear, O earth! For the LORD has spoken: "I have nourished and brought up children, and they have rebelled against Me; The ox knows its owner and the donkey its master's crib; but Israel does not know, my people do not consider." Isaiah 1:2 to 3 (NKJV)* Even the donkey knows where to go.

They have forsaken the LORD, ... they have turned away backward. Isaiah 1:4 (NKJV) In trying to escape, many have turned away backward, "they have forsaken the Lord" they have run to alcohol, drugs, going their own way and doing their own things.

At some point in time, you will need a place to run to, you will need a shelter. If not today, then tomorrow. Everyone – at some time has to have a shelter - when the heat is on, when the battle rages, in the storms of life. All at some time are vulnerable - fiery darts, vicissitudes of life. But there is a safe place, a haven, to run to. *And there shall be a tabernacle for a shadow in the daytime from the heat, and for a place of refuge, and for a covert from storm and from rain.* Isaiah 4:6 There is a place to run to, there is a box to hide in. *The name of the LORD is a strong tower: the righteous runneth into it, and is safe.* Proverbs 18:10

In the most serious, desperate, hopeless situations, hold on to the horns of the altar. Go to the proverbial City of

Refuge. As the songs say, "I go to the rock of my salvation, I go to the stone that the builders rejected."

Be thou my strong habitation, whereunto I may continually resort: thou hast given commandment to save me; for thou art my rock and my fortress. Psalm 71:3

The eternal God is thy refuge, and underneath are the <u>everlasting arms</u>: and he shall thrust out the enemy from before thee; and shall say, Destroy them. Deuteronomy 33:27

The God of my rock; in him will I trust: he is my shield, and the horn of my salvation, my high tower, and my refuge, my saviour; thou savest me from violence. 2 Samuel 22:33

God is our refuge and strength, a very present help in trouble. Therefore will not we fear, though the earth be removed, and though the mountains be carried into the midst of the sea; Though the waters thereof roar and be troubled, though the mountains shake with the swelling thereof. Selah. There is a river, the streams whereof shall make glad the city of God, the holy place of the tabernacles of the most High. God is in the midst of her; she shall not be moved: God shall help her, and that right early. The heathen raged, the kingdoms were moved: he uttered his voice, the earth melted. The LORD of hosts is with us; the God of Jacob is our refuge. Selah. Psalm 46:1-7

Be merciful unto me, O God, be merciful unto me: for my soul trusteth in thee: yea, in the shadow of thy wings will I make my refuge, until these calamities be overpast. Psalm 57:1

And a man shall be as an hiding place from the wind, and a covert from the tempest; as rivers of water in a dry place, as the shadow of a great rock in a weary land. Isaiah 32:2

If you have been running in the wrong direction, today like the prodigal son, like Naomi, make an about face and run in the right direction. The Father will meet you. Always, always.

Some reader today may be struggling today with an impulse, not to run away but just to take a detour, looking for a way out. Where are you going to go? *Cast thy burden upon the LORD, and he shall sustain thee: he shall never suffer the righteous to be moved.* Psalm 55:22 *Trust in him at all times; ye people, pour out your heart before him: God is a refuge for us. Selah.* Psalm 62:8

Others today not literally, not physically but spiritually, mentally, emotionally you have run away from it, you have distanced yourself with drugs and alcohol, with unbiblical responses, searing your conscience, with harmful excursions. You are sojourning, not planning to stay, but caught in a net of your making. Run to Him today. *Come unto me, all ye that labour and are heavy laden, and I will give you rest.* Matthew 11:28 *But they that wait upon the LORD shall renew their strength; they shall mount up with wings as eagles; they shall run, and not be weary; and they shall walk, and not faint.* Isaiah 40:31

Jesus lovingly asks: Will you also run away? Like Peter we reply: To whom should we go? Realize with President Abraham Lincoln: "I have been driven many times to my knees by the overwhelming conviction that I had nowhere else to go.

From the end of the earth will I cry unto thee, when my heart is overwhelmed: lead me to the rock that is higher than I. For thou hast been a shelter for me, and a strong tower from the enemy. I will abide in thy tabernacle for ever: I will trust in the covert of thy wings. Selah. Psalm 61:1-4

Life Application

1. Consider the different excuses or reasons one may have to flee and match the reason to the ones in the Bible who fled:

- Fleeing consequences of past.
- Fleeing responsibilities.
- Fleeing want, famine.
- Fleeing intolerable situation:
- Fleeing Egypt
- Fleeing because of fear, discouragement:
- Fleeing a call of God.

CAIN	PRODIGAL	ISRAELIS
JACOB	DEMAS	ELIJAH
MOSES	NAOMI	JONAH

2. Which of these situations eventually had a good outcome? What was it that brought about the good outcome

3. When can fleeing be a godly response? Are there are times to flee. See John 10:5, 1 Timothy 6:11, 2 Timothy 2:22

NOTES:

ABOUT THE AUTHOR

Mary Wolfe was born and raised in a Pentecostal pastor's home, the daughter of Rev. J. Roy Weidner. She was active in her teenage years in teaching and working in the church. In 1961, she married Evangelist Larry E. Wolfe and joined him in evangelizing in the southeastern United States from 1961-1965. They pastored Camp Eight United Pentecostal Church in central Louisiana and were blessed to serve as home missionaries from 1968-1974, establishing a Christmas for Christ church in Danville, Virginia. In 1974, Larry and Mary returned to Louisiana where they pastored the United Pentecostal Church in Whitehall, Louisiana and then the United Pentecostal Church in Calhoun, Louisiana. During these years of ministry, Mary served on district women's ministry committees and was often a speaker at women's conferences and seminars. She has written for religious publications and has had articles published in the Louisiana District *Challenger* as well as *The Pentecostal Herald, The Conqueror,* and *Word Aflame* Sunday School curriculum.

Mary and Larry have four daughters and five grandchildren whom they love dearly - and whom they consider their greatest achievement.

Mary and Larry have attended The Pentecostals of Alexandria where she has been very active and used extensively as a teacher in many venues. She has been a contributing writer from time-to-time for the *"Weekly Connect"* paper and also The Knowledge Project (Sunday School curriculum). She retired from the federal government as an administrative medical secretary at England Air Force Base Hospital and Veterans Affairs Medical Center in Alexandria, Louisiana.

Trusting God with the Unexplained is her first book to be published, but hopefully will not be her last.

Made in the USA
Coppell, TX
29 January 2023

11920258R00065